An Introduction to Home Education

How to Begin Your Private Homeschool

Original edition by
Susan Beatty and Karen Woodfin Middleton

Edited by Susan Beatty, Karen Koch, Susan K. Stewart,
and Mary Schofield

Contributing authors: Sandra Cruz, Jim Davis, Roy M. Hanson, Jr.,
Mary Schofield, Susan K. Stewart, Evella Troutt, Philip Troutt

Published by
Christian Home Educators Press
A Division of Christian Home Educators Association of California, Inc.
12440 E. Firestone Blvd., Suite 311

© 1983, 2004, 2005, 2006, 2007, 2009, 2012, 2014
by Christian Home Educators Association of California, Inc.

Twelfth Edition Revised, 2014

ISBN 978-0-9770707-9-4

The information in this manual is not intended to be legal advice. For advice on legal matters, the reader should consult an attorney.

Table of Contents

Preface

As homeschooling has grown throughout the last three decades, so have the number of books and resources. But one thing remains constant: the need for clear and simple guidelines to help the beginner get started in homeschooling. The beginner often finds herself lost in a long list of so-called self-help books about homeschooling and bogged down in the many details and opinions within those books. This doesn't even count the thousands of websites that can overpower someone just getting started. Where can an inquirer or a beginner start that doesn't seem so overwhelming?

Since the first edition in 1983, we have believed the best place to start is this book, *An Introduction to Home Education*. With each edition the book has grown and been updated, but we have resisted the urge to make this the "everything you ever wanted to know about homeschooling book," believing that would be too overwhelming to someone just embarking on this great adventure. So while this is the new and greatly improved 12th Edition Revised with updated information on the laws, filing an affidavit, recordkeeping, resources and more, it remains the must-have basic course in home education.

I would like to thank Karen Woodfin Middleton for "giving birth" to the original manuscript of this book. It was then that I came along to edit it, adding this and that, and expanding it over the years.

The new 12th Edition is the result of a gargantuan amount of rewriting, revising, reorganizing, and re-design by Susan Stewart and Mary Schofield. The 12th Edition Revised is the work of Susan Stewart and Karen Koch.

There are many other people who have contributed to this work over the years as well, particularly Pam Piepenburg, for devising most of the record keeping forms; Philip and Evella Troutt, for contributing written portions; Jim Davis, Roy M. Hanson, J. Michael Smith, and Mary Schofield for their extensive legislative and legal contributions; Marty Molina of GraphicType, for the completed cover design; and Corey and Bill Wylde, for their printing expertise.

We dedicate this book to the thousands of families who have followed God's call to direct the education of their children through homeschooling, to the thousands of families that we have been able to help through the ministry of Christian Home Educators Association of California, and to you, the new homeschooler, who is on the brink of an exciting adventure. God speed.

Thank you all!

--Susan Beatty

October, 2012

Abbreviations

Just like any job or organization, homeschooling is rife with acronyms and unique terms. While these are included in the glossary, common abbreviations are listed here for easy reference as you read.

CDE   California Department of Education

CHEA   Christian Home Educators Association of California

E.C.   California Education Code

FPM   Family Protection Ministries

HSC   California Health and Safety Code

HSLDA   Home School Legal Defense Association

ISP   Independent Study Program

PSA   Private School Affidavit

PSP   Private School Satellite Program

Chapter One
Getting Started

Quick Start

You may be starting to homeschool sometime during the school year without having the opportunity to do all the preparation recommended in this book. If you are in that situation, read this section first. The suggestions here will get you started teaching your children while you set up your homeschool program.

One issue that must be handled immediately is taking care of school attendance so that your children won't be charged with truancy. In most districts, unexcused absences are considered truancy on the third day. However, some schools verify all absences starting with day one. So you must take care of attendance issues before you even begin working with the children on their first day of homeschool.

If your children's previous school has a call-in for absence procedure, follow their procedure. You don't need to tell them your children are not returning as long as the school will receive a letter of withdrawal by the third day of absence. Letters of withdrawal are covered later in this chapter.

The key steps for beginning your homeschool are covered in chapters one and two, so make it a priority to read these two chapters on the first day your children are out of their old school.

But what do you do with the children while you are taking care of these preliminary issues?

The first thing to remember is you don't have to start right off with a full school day. Often children need time to adjust from going to school each day to being in the more relaxed atmosphere of home. So you may want to plan to spend each morning of your first week getting set up, and wait until the afternoon to teach. It's even fine to have your children take the whole first day or two off of school entirely so that you can focus on the set-up for your new program. If they're old enough, the children can help set up your new homeschool as their first assignment.

It is also fine for your homeschool adventure to begin with simply reading for the first week or two. Read the Bible as a family, with older children each taking a turn. Some of those classics that you remember from high school are more exciting when read aloud.

Set a routine for your days. This doesn't mean you need a strict schedule, although children who have been in traditional classrooms for a number of years may be "programmed" to a strict schedule: It's 9 a.m., we do math. Making a list of school tasks you want to accomplish for the week may be enough of a lesson plan.

Beginning Lesson Ideas

While your children are decompressing from traditional school structure, you can work through this book, making plans and taking care of business. Below are ideas for your children during decompression time.

Language Arts

Reading

Establish a routine of reading from the Bible together. Older children can take a few minutes to write their thoughts in their journals.

Pick a book to read together. Little ones may draw quietly while you or one of the older children reads aloud.

Writing

Copy work: Have your children copy from the Bible or the book you are reading.

Narrative: Ask the children to tell stories back to you, or write a summary of the story. Small children can draw a picture about the story, and you write their sentences to go with the picture.

Composition and Creative Writing: Write their own story. For younger children, you write the story exactly as they tell it, and they illustrate it.

Give your child a picture to write a story from. Make a book with your child's words and pictures. Or, get pictures books from the library and write the story.

Write a letter to Grandma, to a missionary your church supports, or even to the president.

Math

Cooking: Not only does having your children fix meals teach a life skill, but many math lessons are included. Fractions and multiplication come to mind right away. Additionally, you can teach children to budget money and shop carefully as part of meal planning.

Math Facts: Everyone can benefit from review of math facts. You can make flash cards for your younger children. If you have older children, have them make the flash cards and do the review with the little ones. All children will benefit.

Games: Many board games have a mathematics component. For example, Monopoly™ and Life™ require money skills, while Yahtzee™ requires lots of addition.

Science

Just look outside and you will find plenty of science to keep you busy. Watch the weather, using a calendar to track it. Compare what happens with what was predicted on television or an internet site. Older children can research the science of weather predictions. Bird watching, bug watching, leaf collections, or rock collections can become long-term science projects or even lifelong hobbies.

History

Reading the Bible is the foundation for other history lessons. Reading historical novels will also give a sense of a specific time period. Does your child have a particular interest like knights in shining armor or royalty? Go to the library and select books to read together or individually. Let your child pick a project to do, such as make a miniature village or draw the family tree of the Tudors or even your own family tree.

Physical Education

Most children are physically active by nature. You don't need a specific P.E. program. Bicycle riding, jumping rope, and playing on the swing set provide plenty of physical activity.

Field trips are legitimate educational activities. Go to museums, libraries, zoos, art shows, or wherever there is something of interest to your family. Many homeschool groups sponsor group field trips with lower admission prices.

These activities can continue to the end of the school year, giving you time to research learning styles and teaching approaches. You may also want to plan to attend a convention near you to learn more about homeschooling and look at the materials available to you. CHEA hosts two conventions each year offering diverse workshops and large exhibit halls. Check the web site for details: www.cheaofca.org.

As you and your children settle into being at home together, you can start establishing a routine that works for your family. Begin slowly. Add one textbook or subject at a time. Establish your family's school routine. Enjoy the freedom of having a school schedule that fits your family's needs. And, you don't have to do math at 9 a.m.

For a free Emergency Learning Plan, see Ambleside Online, www.amblesideonline.org. Click "Ambleside Online Curriculum" and scroll to the article "AO-Help Emergency Lesson Plan."

Making the Decision

Consider the Biblical Admonitions

Your first consideration should be "What does the Bible say about child training and education?" To summarize, the Bible says children do not belong to the state, but to God who has entrusted them to you as parents. You are responsible for educating your children in wisdom and training, for God has set the home, not the school, as the center of learning. The church and school are extensions of the home and the parents. True knowledge and wisdom come not from the world but from God through His Word, which is the measure of all things and the foundation of true education. The purpose of education is to train the child to be a faithful servant of God, to seek holiness, and to be equipped (i.e., competent) to fulfill God's great commission.

Consider the Law

While the Bible is our authority concerning the responsibility of our children, we must be aware of the law and be in subjection to the authority of the law to the best of our ability and where it does not conflict with God's laws. Education for Christian children is a First Amendment freedom of religion issue. However, the U.S. Constitution left education within the realm of the states for specific statutes. Therefore, not only do we need to know what our federal Constitution says, we also need to be aware of the requirements in the Education Code and other state laws. If these laws coincide with Scripture, we are free without further thought to follow our desired course of action. However, if the laws are in conflict with what we sincerely believe God has commanded us to do, we follow God's laws. Unfortunately, God's laws and man's laws are usually not so clearly on opposite ends of the spectrum, causing us to pray, seek wisdom, search the Scriptures, examine the law and our conscience, and only then make a right decision.

Consider Your Children

If your children are preschool age, you are no doubt concerned about where and how they will develop to their greatest potential. You need to decide whether that development has the greater chance of happening in your home or in a school. You will hear logical-sounding arguments from advocates of both positions. In the end, however, you will have to act with godly discernment.

If your children are already in school, you may be dissatisfied in some way and looking for an alternative. Your question now is, "What can I do to change this unsatisfactory situation?"

Carefully think through all your choices, pro and con, until one choice stands out as the best answer. If the best answer appears to be to bring your children home and educate them yourself, then you need to go on to the next consideration.

Consider Your Family and Lifestyle

How you view the goals, purposes, role of the family, and your lifestyle are crucial to the ultimate success of your home education experience. Is the purpose of the family to love, nurture, and protect its members? To foster respect for all, even the children? Is your home a place of serenity and beauty? Beauty that doesn't come from a high standard of living but, from a love for God's world and a desire to make others feel special. Does each family member feel free to be himself?

Is the goal of the family to give every material advantage or every spiritual advantage? Are you willing to learn better organization, discipline, and consistency?

Does your lifestyle exhibit a vision for the role of motherhood and fatherhood? Are your children important enough to you to spend quantity and quality time with them?

Consider Yourself

Bringing your children home or keeping them home from the beginning will, at the very least, set you firmly apart from the average family. In addition, it may mean a drastic change in your lifestyle. It may also set you up as the object of criticism and ridicule. It may even cause you to have to defend your actions. Consequently, you should be sure that educating your children is a strong conviction.

Famous Homeschoolers

Many famous achievers never went to school or began during adolescence or later. Of course, we would not suggest all of these as models of Christian character; nevertheless, we can learn something from their lives.

Presidents
George Washington
John Quincy Adams
William Henry Harrison
Abraham Lincoln
James Madison
Franklin Delano
   Roosevelt
Woodrow Wilson

Painters
Claude Monet
Leonardo da Vinci
Andrew & Jamie Wyeth

Preachers
John the Baptist
Phillip Melanchthon

Generals
Stonewall Jackson
Robert E. Lee
Douglas MacArthur
Moses
George Patton

Scientists
George Washington
   Carver
Pierre Curie

Inventors
Alexander Graham Bell
Thomas Edison
Cyrus McCormick
Wright Brothers

Educators
Frank Vandiver
   (Texas A&M)
Fred Terman
   (Stanford)

Writers
Hans Christian
   Anderson
Pearl S. Buck
Agatha Christie
Charles Dickens
George Bernard Shaw
Brette Harte

Statesmen
Konrad Adenauer
Winston Churchill
Benjamin Franklin
Patrick Henry
William Penn

Others
Charlie Chaplin (actor)
George Rogers Clark
   (explorer)
Andrew Carnegie
   (industrialist)
William F. Buckley, Jr.
   (journalist)
John Burroughs
   (naturalist)
Albert Schweitzer
   (physician)
Noel Coward
   (playwright)
Tamara McKinney
   (world cup skier)

Pros and Cons

Here are some of our pros and cons regarding the decision to homeschool. Add to this list your own thoughts.

PRO

- Teacher is nicer
- Promotes family unity
- Children are more relaxed
- Less damage to self-concept
- Less costly than private school
- More time for community service
- Teaches children to think creatively
- More time for extracurricular activities
- God can totally be the center of family life
- Can develop in areas not covered in school
- Fewer illnesses and lower health care costs
- Teach as slowly or quickly as individually necessary
- Teaches self-discipline, commitment & self-sacrifice
- Better retention of subjects because there is no promotion until subject is mastered
- Can take advantage of learning opportunities no matter what time of day, week, or year
- _____
  _____
- _____
  _____

CON

- More costly than public school
- Takes extra work and initiative (homeschooling is not easy)
- Need to learn self-discipline and organizational skills
- Adjustment to a different lifestyle
- Mother (and sometimes father) has less time for self
- Standards of household neatness may have to be lowered for a time, especially in families with babies and preschoolers
- Possible estrangement from disapproving relatives and friends
- Chance of harassment from school officials
- _____
  _____
- _____
  _____

Philosophy of Education

Philosophy of education is a semester long course at most colleges. And that can be intimidating. Rather than thinking of philosophy, think of the question, "Why home educate?" The answer to this question will help you determine all aspects of your home education program.

Why Educate?

Every system of education, whether public, private, Christian, democratic, communist, home or other, has three elements which constitute its essential nature. These elements are: 1) philosophy, 2) curriculum, and 3) methods. The order of listing is neither accidental nor arbitrary, but reflects the true relationship between the three. Regrettably, most homeschoolers fail to grasp this fundamental relationship and begin and end their consideration of education with curriculum. To attempt to make wise decisions about curriculum without clearly asking and answering the basic questions as to the purpose and goals of education is to set out on a journey with no destination.

Most of us take for granted that our children must be educated and it is simply a question of how to go about it. We have some general concept of what constitutes education, based primarily on our own experience. What we fail to realize is that our experience was the expression of a philosophy of education that may or may not be consistent with our own.

There is a basic question we must all ask if we are going to succeed in our educational endeavors: "Why educate?" What is, or should be, our motivation for undertaking any system of instruction? The world's answers to this question are well known: to get a "better" job, to make more money, to be a "good" citizen. But are these answers appropriate for one proceeding from a biblical perspective?

Philosophy is the "Why" of education. It is primary and causative. It gives direction and establishes the framework upon which the structure of education is built. A philosophy of education is itself determined by our philosophy of God, Man, and Government. (Government? Yes, government — meaning control or direction, who or what is in control.) An educational system based on a denial of God will be structured differently from and will produce a very different result from one which assumes God as the starting point for all true knowledge. In the same way, a system which views man as nothing more than a high order evolutionary being, whose only value is to serve society, will be different from one which views man as created in the image of and existing to fulfill the plan and purpose of an eternal God. A system which believes that individual men are incapable of directing or governing their own lives will have a different goal in mind and will pursue different methods in developing an educational system.

Curriculum answers the question "What" is to be taught in order to achieve the goals established by the answers to "Why." It must be consistent with and subordinate to philosophy. Curriculum which has been developed to support a worldly view of God, Man, and Government can hardly be expected to fulfill goals that result from a Godly perspective. Even Christian curriculums will reflect the particular philosophy of the person or persons who create them.

Methods are the "How" of education and, like curriculum, are derived from the primary position of philosophy. Methods must be compatible with that philosophy in order to have an integrated system. Anyone who has trained for a state teaching credential has learned teaching methods based on a secular philosophy of education. That is, a view of man as a biological, cosmological accident who must be "conditioned" to behave in certain ways. These methods are concerned with the external nature, or behavior, of man, rather than his internal nature or character. Those who have been trained by the state must be careful when attempting to apply those methods to their Christian homeschool, and others must be careful when asking the counsel of such individuals.

Each child is unique and has a special place in God's eternal plan. No plan of education will be exactly the same for any two children, even in the same family. Parents must take the time to answer the fundamental question of "Why" for each child prior to beginning home education or choosing curriculum in order to make wise choices.

By Philip Troutt. Reprinted with permission.

The Purpose and Goals of Education

Now that you are thinking in vague terms about the "Why" of education, let's get specific. What are some of the purposes and goals of education?

You begin by regarding the foundation of education as truth and that the foundation of truth is the Bible (John 17:17, Isa 8:20, Col 2:8, Ps 111:10). The Bible tells us the goal of education is to "bring ... every thought captive to the obedience of Christ" (II Cor 10:5). Augustine defined Christian education as, "to think God's thoughts after Him." In other words, the goal of Christian education is to cause the Christian person to be growing in grace and the knowledge of Christ, pursuing godliness of character and action (II Tim 3:17), and preparing him to exercise that knowledge in service (I Chr 28:9).

What about academics? Academics are secondary to godly character values, but we are nevertheless to gain dominion over all academic disciplines in order to bring glory to God, the creator of the disciplines.

When you know where you are going (i.e., godliness of character and action, mastery of the basic academic disciplines), you can decide how far you have to go to get there. Whatever is lacking in the student's character according to the Scriptures is where you begin his education. It's like using a road map. If you don't know where you are going or where you are now, any road will get you there. But when you know your destination and your present location, you can begin thinking about how you are going to get there. As with most destinations, there are probably several modes of transportation and several routes from which to choose. In the next section we will summarize the philosophy that will affect your mode of transportation (educational system).

The Role of Home Education

It may appear that the purposes and goals of Christian education can be carried out with equal effectiveness in a traditional Christian school. Why then would you consider home education to be the best vehicle? To be convinced you are being called into home education, you must consider this question well.

As previously mentioned, God has through His Word given the parents the responsibility of educating their children. While parts of the job can be delegated to others (i.e., campus schools or hired tutors), the ultimate responsibility is still the parents'. Can you carry out this responsibility more effectively by delegating the job to others and conducting quality control from afar, or by doing the job yourself? Throughout history the home and family have been the basic unit of society. It has only been within the last century that the home is no longer considered the primary place for earning a living, education, birth, death, etc. For centuries, the home proved to be an effective place from which to conduct these important areas of our life. Fundamentally, that has not changed.

Earlier in this chapter you were introduced to some practical reasons for choosing home education. Putting them into the perspective of a philosophy of Christian home education, we can summarize as follows. The home is the center of love, warmth, and security. It is a familiar place, lacking some of the pressures of the outside world that children would be better off without until mature enough to handle them. It should be a place where the child is accepted as who, in the sight of God, he really is, and where he can be nurtured and encouraged by those who love him best. It is viewing the role of parents as servants of Jesus Christ, raising their children in a manner that will best meet the needs of the individual child. It is not necessarily duplicating the methods of the local school, but, as Susan Schaeffer Macaulay says in her book, *For the Children's Sake*, "Education is people living life, side by side, preparing a child for the whole of life." As she quotes from Charlotte Mason, "Education is a life."

Writing Your Philosophy of Education

Now that you know why you should have a philosophy of home education, it is time to begin writing it. This process is not an individual process. Husband and wife should work together, sharing their opinions and ideas. It is also not a quick-study project; it may take you several weeks or months. If you are already homeschooling, don't stop just because you don't have a written statement of why you are doing this. While your children are doing their schoolwork, you can be doing yours.

Once you write your home education philosophy, you will have a better understanding of what it is you want to impart to your children. You may also see why particular methods and curriculum aren't working. Please don't feel you have failed your children if what you are using is not working. Consider what changes need to be made to bring your curriculum and teaching methods into line with your educational philosophy. Then make changes accordingly and move forward.

If someone questions your decision to teach your children at home, knowing your educational philosophy will help you to answer questions without questioning yourself. It is also helpful to have your statement of philosophy handy for those days when you are wondering why you are doing this.

Read your philosophy to your children once in a while so when they wonder why you have

Questions to Build a Philosophy of Education

It is a good idea to find Scripture references to support your beliefs.

• **What is your worldview?**

This is your framework that helps you understand society, your place in it, and helps you with critical decisions. It is your picture of the world and how you respond to it. Your worldview is the foundation of your philosophy of life, which now includes home education.

• **What is your belief about God?**

Do you believe in God? Describe God as you understand Him. This is a good study question for the entire family. If you have trouble with this, seek advice from a trusted Christian.

• **What is your belief about humans?**

Do you believe humans were created or evolved? What is the relationship between human beings and God? Are humans inherently good or evil?

— More on next page.

More Philosophy-building Questions

•**What do you believe about God's Word?**

Do you think it is completely true without error? Or, a series of mythological stories?

•**What is the definition of education?**

What does the Bible say about teaching children? Try not to think in the traditional terms of education, i.e.: classrooms, tests, lesson plans, etc. Start with a standard definition from a dictionary, such as this one from the Webster's 1828 American Christian Dictionary:

The bringing up, as of a child, instruction; formation of manners. Education comprehends all that series of instruction and discipline which is intended to enlighten the understanding, correct the temper, and form the manners and habits of youth, and fit them for usefulness in their future stations. To give children a good education in manners, arts and science, is important; to give them a religious education is indispensable; and an immense responsibility rests on parents and guardians who neglect these duties.

•**What is wisdom and knowledge?**

Start with the dictionary definition. Include what God has to say about wisdom and knowledge? Determine how these concepts fit into your home education experience.

•**What is your belief about parental responsibility? About children?**

Once you have an education philosophy, you may want to apply the answers to these questions to the individual subjects.

By Susan K. Stewart. Reprinted with permission.

chosen this course of action they will understand and learn the godly principles behind raising children.

If you skimmed over (or skipped completely) the previous sections on philosophy, stop now and go back, reading carefully and thoughtfully.

In order to begin your homeschool with a solid foundation, you must think through your philosophy, verbalize it, and commit it to paper. The result should be a document that is kept with your school files, ready to be used if your school is questioned. Verbalizing what you have learned and your thoughts about that, internalizes it for yourself. When asked, it will be easier to give an account of what you believe and why. More importantly, you shouldn't purchase curriculum until you have settled these issues and decided upon your approach to home education.

Legal Foundations

The Right to "Direct the Education and Upbringing" of Your Children

The fundamental right of parents to direct the education and upbringing of their children is guaranteed by the First, Ninth, and Fourteenth Amendments to the Constitution of the United States. The Constitution does not specifically state that parents have the right to raise their children, much less to homeschool them. However, when there have been legal challenges, the Supreme Court has interpreted the Constitution to guarantee this, relying on the First Amendment's right to freedom of speech and religion, the Fourth Amendment's protection from unreasonable searches and seizure, and the Ninth Amendment's clarification that there are additional rights to those spelled out specifically within the Constitution.

Since the U.S. Constitution is the highest law, all lesser laws must be consistent with the Constitution or they risk being declared invalid. Thus, since the Constitution guarantees the right to raise one's children, no state or local law may deny that right.

While it is not necessary to know all the legal cases, an introduction to them will help you understand your fundamental right to raise your family according to your beliefs, and will help you be better positioned to protect that right. The next section summarizes some of the important cases and the battle that early homeschoolers fought and won to protect your right to homeschool today.

Homeschool History

"Children at risk." "Students hunted down." "Parents arrested and jailed." Sound like headlines about a third-world country or a secretive cult? They are not. These are headlines about home educators — home educators in the United States. Headlines like these, followed by articles about the perils of home education, appeared in the media just a mere two decades ago, some less than 10 years ago, when homeschooling was considered new.

But home education is certainly not a new phenomenon. One hundred years ago, Calvert School began their Home Instruction Department. Prior to that, informal home instruction was the norm.

By the 1940s and 1950s, as free government schools became more prevalent, it didn't seem necessary, or even desirable, to keep children at home under the tutelage of their parents. But, as free education became worth what it cost — nothing — parents sought to take back control of their families.

In the 1970s, homeschooling was thought to be an outgrowth of the freedom, peace, and love movement. But it wasn't long before Christian families were embracing this alternative method to train their children. By the early 1980s, as home education became more popular, opposition began in earnest.

CHEA of California was founded in 1982. On its heels, in 1983, at least eight other state home education organizations were founded, the first issue of *The Teaching Home Magazine* was published, and Home School Legal Defense Association was founded. Montana adopted a home education/private school law. And the Supreme Court ruled Georgia's compulsory school law unconstitutional. Thus began an educational revolution called home education.

Most of the resistance to homeschooling was from public school administrators who had little understanding of the rights of parents. Today it may be hard to imagine resistance that is more than having to answer an inquiring phone call, but not so in 1983.

Chris Klicka, the senior counsel of HSLDA, talks about it: "Fear, describes those early days. People were afraid."

At that time California was considered a fairly "safe" state in which to home educate because compulsory education laws were satisfied through the private school exemption rather than through a specific homeschool law. However, even here families were teaching their children behind drawn curtains and not going outside during school hours.

In other states, parents were being prosecuted and convicted for taking a stand against compulsory education laws that limited their freedom to educate their children in the way God told them to. North Dakota was such a hotbed of legal fires that one mother, upon moving to North Dakota, wrote, "We had already decided to NEVER tell anyone else that we were homeschooling." And, "We were too paranoid to contact other North Dakota homeschoolers."

During the early eighties, families in that state were being prosecuted and convicted for violation of compulsory education laws. After a series of appeals, in 1986 the State Supreme Court ruled against these families. In 1987 two of the families were tried again and again lost. And more and more families were being charged.

In 1989, homeschoolers from 11 states, including California, went to Bismarck for the "Bismarck Tea Party," flooding the legislators' offices with tea bags saying, "The consent of the governed for homeschoolers, too." It was that year, after a six-year struggle, that North Dakota's governor signed their state's homeschool law.

At the same time, to the south in Iowa, officials not only went after homeschooling families, they attacked private day schools as well. Several fathers and a pastor were sent to jail for violating compulsory education laws.

One pioneer home educator stated, "During these earlier years, I attended meetings of homeschooling families who knew they were unlawful in their homeschooling programs, and who had 'underground' contingency plans to remove children — and often, homeschooling mothers, too — from the confines of Iowa in order to escape Iowa authorities."

Legal battles were heating up in California as well. Over the next few years, there would be major cases, but one in 1989,

People v. Darrah and Black, set a precedent to protect home-based private schools in California. The municipal court ruled that the terms "persons capable of teaching" and "private full-time day school," which were part of our private school law, were unconstitutionally vague and could not be enforced. This ruling still hasn't been challenged today.

In 1995, three California truancy cases were brought to court. All were cleared by relying on the private school exemption.

After 1996, when the eight-year long *DeJonge* case in Michigan was settled, homeschooling court battles quieted down and didn't reach far beyond a few individual families. Homeschooling seemed to be an accepted educational alternative. Homeschooling was acceptable.

For Californians, the quiet ended in 2008. This time a non-homeschool legal situation had an impact on all homeschoolers in the state. The Court of Appeal for the Second Appellate District in Los Angeles ruled in the *In re Rachel L.* case, stating that parents who did not hold a teaching credential could not legally homeschool their children.

Because *In re Rachel L.* was a juvenile dependency case, the records were sealed; there was no indication outside the court that homeschooling was at issue. Major homeschool organizations, including CHEA of California, HomeSchool Association of California, California Homeschool Network, Family Protection Ministries, and HSLDA, worked together to petition the court for a rehearing. And six months after the initial ruling, the justices reversed their original ruling.

Four years, six years, eight years. That's how long parents were willing to fight for the principle of parents' right to direct the education of their children without government interference or government involvement. These parents were willing to put everything on the line for the right to freely teach children at home.

This brief history shows that the freedom to homeschool was fought for, and it was a freedom that wasn't easily won. It has been a battle.

And the battle continues. It's a battle that we know God has ultimately already won, but the enemy, Satan, won't give up easily.

For example, notice the misinformation in a Bakersfield newspaper report in 2005: " ... Kern County School District Assistant Superintendent, Bud Burrow ... when asked how many children in the county were homeschooled replied, 'We wouldn't have a clue, because homeschooling is outside the legal and proper way of doing things. California is a compulsory attendance state, and it's illegal. It's either home or school — it's not meant to be both.'" The article goes on to state "the legal way to homeschool is through a public school independent study program, a charter school or via tutoring by a certified teacher."

Another common battle is the government schools' constant attempts to "help" through public independent study and charter schools. The invitation to bring government education into homes is seen by some as an indication of the public schools' acceptance of home education. In fact, it is the antithesis of what the early home educating families fought for.

Legislative battles can be even subtler. New laws are typically not aimed directly at home education. Instead, they creep in with more government education. Full day kindergarten (AB 2024) and Universal Preschool (Proposition 82) could easily become mandatory school years in the not-too-distant future. As the government mandates more and more new education programs, more oversight will be demanded, potentially including oversight of private homeschools. The new century is like a time warp for the veterans who fought the good fight for the freedom and choices now available. They see history repeating itself. The government camel is putting his nose under the edge of the tent of home education.

For a detailed time line of important court cases, go to www.hslda.org/about/history.asp.

By Susan K. Stewart. Reprinted with permission.

California's Compulsory Attendance Law

In California, there is no legally defined entity called a "homeschool." Instead of having a separate homeschool law, California is one of 12 states in which homeschoolers operate as private schools. Private schools can be legally established and operated on traditional school campuses, of course, but they can just as legally be established in homes. The law does not specify a location. Thus, wherever your school operates, you are technically a "private school," and you should use that term when dealing with government officials or when handling legal issues. "Homeschooling" is only a colloquial term adopted by homeschoolers to distinguish their programs from campus-based ones. The law makes no such distinction — all private schools are governed by the same laws.

Compulsory Attendance Laws

Under the California Education Code, all children between the ages of six and 18 must attend a public full-time day school unless they are exempted (E.C. § 48200). The four most common exemptions which apply to homeschoolers are:

1. Start your own private school.

2. Enroll in Private School Satellite Program (PSP)

3. Use a tutor.

4. Enroll in a charter school or independent study through the public school.

Each of these options will be discussed separately below.

1. Starting Your Own Private School

Home educators may legally establish private schools in their own homes. These schools must comply with the same laws that apply to all private schools, including filing a Private School Affidavit each year. The requirements are discussed in detail in chapter two.

2. Enrolling in a PSP

A PSP must meet the same legal requirements as all other private schools, so before enrolling, you should become familiar with the requirements discussed in chapter two and ask questions to make sure the program is in compliance. PSPs may be composed entirely of homeschoolers or may be an extension program of a campus-based private school.

3. Using a Private Tutor

Private tutoring requires a California credentialed teacher. The credential must be for the appropriate grade level and teaching must be in the courses of study required in the public schools. Tutoring must be done for at least three hours a day for at least 175 days per year. (E.C. § 48224)

Most homeschool parents who have teaching credentials choose to operate as private schools even though they qualify as tutors. The reason is the time requirement. As will be discussed in chapter two, private schools have no set requirement for teaching a particular number of hours or days, while private tutors do. Thus the day-to-day recordkeeping is easier for a private school.

4. Enrolling in a Charter School or Public School ISP

When your children attend a charter school or public school ISP, they are not "exempt" from the compulsory attendance law, they are in compliance with it. This is because these programs are public schools. When your children enroll, they are public school students.

State law requires that the students in these programs must be under the "exclusive control of the officers of the public schools." (E.C. § 47612(a)) This means that while parents may be involved in the day-to-day supervision of the child's schoolwork, all final decisions are made by the public school official in charge. Additionally, a signed agreement is required specifying minimum requirements. Also, regular standardized tests are required and specified academic progress must be maintained or the program risks losing funding. Because families who choose this option relinquish some of the freedom and right to direct their children's education, it's not recommended. For more details see "Why Charter Schools Won't Work for Christians" on page 40.

Age of Enrollment

Note that kindergarten attendance is not required in California. Also, while the law requires students to be enrolled in school upon turning six years old, most schools start in the fall rather than on a particular child's birthday. So public school districts look at the age of the child when school begins in the fall and they have traditionally allowed enrollment in first grade as long as the child will be six years old by December 2. However, a new program in many districts requires a child to be six by September 1 in order to enroll in first grade. Because of this inconsistency, enrollment in your private school in August or September of the year in which your child turns six is probably the easiest way to meet the compulsory attendance requirement.

Out-of-state Programs

Families enrolled in out-of-state schools or programs are still required by state law to be enrolled in a California private school (home-based or PSP) with a California address for its location. Thus, families who use these programs must have their children dual-enrolled in both the out-of-state program *and* in a private school in California. Of course, out-of-state curriculum sources are fine to use, but if the program you're considering requires enrollment in their program, be aware that you'll still need to comply with California compulsory attendance laws by enrolling in an in-state program.

Because out-of-state schools are not recognized as meeting compulsory attendance requirements in California, it is unwise and unnecessary to voluntarily mention enrollment in one. It is not illegal to be enrolled in an out-of-state program, it just won't meet compulsory attendance requirements. So feel free to enroll your children if you want, just remember that you're using it as a source of curriculum or services, not as a means of legal compliance with the compulsory attendance law.

More about Homeschool Programs

Just as there is no one way to teach, there is no one education program. In additional to establishing your own private school, other options are available.

Distance Learning Programs or Correspondence Schools

Distance learning program is the modern label for the concept previously known as correspondence schools. These programs offer curriculum, testing, recordkeeping, and monitoring of schoolwork. The parent usually submits a report of the child's progress on a regular basis along with samples of work.

Some distance schools will try to help you deal with authorities if necessary. However, their success record has been limited.

The State of California does not recognize out-of-state schools as private schools. HSLDA advises that the strongest legal position for the homeschooler is to establish a private school in the home or enroll the child in a private school satellite program (PSP) located within the State of California, and then use the distance learning program just as a source of curriculum and help for the teacher. Since most PSPs do not require the use of a particular curriculum, you should be able to enroll in a PSP and still use the program and curriculum provided by the distance learning or correspondence school. However, be sure to ask what the PSP's policy is before enrolling your child.

Distance learning or correspondence programs are an alternative for families who feel they need help and the extra discipline of having someone to whom they must be accountable. There is not as much personal involvement with an out-of-state program; however, as there is with other alternatives.

Out-of-state schools should not request cum files from public schools since California does not recognize such schools as valid for student attendance purposes. You, or the administrator of the California-based PSP in which you're enrolled, should request the records.

PSP Without Campus

The PSP without a campus is a program geared specifically toward home-educating families. The administrator files one private school affidavit for the entire school, and sets up the program and requirements.

In general, PSPs offer recordkeeping, accountability, encouragement, and student interaction (holiday programs, field trips, special projects, etc.). Generally registrations and tuition fees are very modest compared to campus-based private schools. Because these programs vary widely in their services, check each school's requirements carefully, making sure it offers the services and requirements appropriate for your family.

PSP with Campus-based Private School

In the PSP with campus, your child is officially enrolled in a traditional private full-time day school and may participate in school activities; however, the student's classroom is at home. The private school's teachers often guide the homeschooling parent by in-home visits, helping with lesson plans, evaluating the child's progress, etc. Tuition may be less than for the school's on-campus program, but is typically more than for a PSP without campus.

If you have children below the age of six or eight (and sometimes even age 10) and believe in delayed formal academics, be sure the school understands your philosophy of early childhood education and your desire to keep your younger children out of pressurized, formal academics. Have a clear understanding with them at the outset about what they will or will not expect out of your young child. The most satisfactory arrangement is usually when the PSP administrator is also a homeschool parent.

Public School ISP

Some counties have ISPs specifically for homeschoolers. Some families have reported good experience and have appreciated

ISP or PSP?

You may have heard the term "ISP." Public school ISPs are governed by Education Code §§51745 and 51746. The view of the California Department of Education (CDE) is that independent study is a public school program which must be supervised by a credentialed teacher employed by the public school district.

This view was expressed by the CDE in 2008: "[A] private school may *not* offer instruction through 'independent study' and a child enrolled in a private school [ISP] ... would not qualify for the exemption from public school attendance" [emphasis in original].

In response to CDE's published opinion, HSLDA, CHEA, and other state homeschool organizations have recommended that private schools with homeschool programs use the term Private School Satellite Program (PSP).

the use of public school facilities and equipment. However, we urge you to completely think through your reasons for homeschooling and your philosophy of Christian education. Since public schools are prohibited from offering or allowing religious education within their programs, it's unlikely that the goals of Christian homeschool parents will be compatible. Some programs have promised non-interference to begin with, only to add more and more restrictions each year. Request to have the program's policies in writing.

Most school districts require you to use state approved texts and give them to you free. While you may use Christian materials that you purchase on your own after school hours, just as you could if your students attended any school, state law prohibits use of Christian-based curriculum for credit in the public schools.

If your child is enrolled in a public school ISP, you will not be eligible for HSLDA membership while in the public school ISP. Additionally, you will be placing your homeschooling under the authority of the public school system over which you have no control.

Charter School

The homeschooled pupil may enroll in a charter school offering home study. (E.C. § 47600 et al.) We cannot recommend this option. The following article briefly details some of the problems with charter school. It is available as a separate brochure from CHEA. Additionally, CHEA carries a booklet which explains each issue in greater detail.

Why Charter Schools Won't Work for Christians

What is a Charter School?

"A charter school is a public school and may provide instruction in any of grades K-12. A charter school is usually created or organized by a group of teachers, parents and community leaders or a community-based organization, and is usually sponsored by an existing local public school board or county board of education. Specific goals and operating procedures for the charter school are detailed in an agreement (or "charter") between the sponsoring board and charter organizers." California Department of Education. "Charter Schools: Q & A." www.cde.ca.gov/charter/qanda/. October 1999.

The majority of charter schools in California are classroom-based, with children going to a school site each school day. This paper focuses on charter schools which enroll homeschoolers. These programs use a variety of titles: homeschooling; independent study; distance learning; virtual, on-line, cyber, or computer-based schools; co-op teaching; correspondence; work study; or home study. What these "non-classroom based" charter schools have in common is that the student completes most of his schooling without attending a classroom.

> For what shall it profit a man, if he shall gain the whole world, and lose his own soul? Or what shall a man give in exchange for his soul?
>
> Mark 8:36-37

Christian Children Need Christian Education

Just as the Christian life cannot be lived only on Sundays, while ignoring God the rest of the week, so Christian education cannot occur in a void apart from the other school subjects. God is the God of science, history, literature, arts, mathematics, and all other subjects. Instruction in all of these areas must point to Him and to His precepts. This cannot happen in a charter school.

Charter Schools Cannot Offer a Christian Education

The law clearly prohibits religious instruction in all public schools, including charter schools: no "sectarian or denominational doctrine [shall] be taught, or instruction thereon be permitted, directly or indirectly" in public schools. (California Constitution, Article IX, Section 8)

Some charter school administrators claim that parents may teach their own children religious doctrine whether they are in a charter school or not. This is true only in the sense that it is true for parents of any public school student. They may pray with him each morning before sending him off to school, they may teach Bible before or after school, and they may take him to church each Sunday. However, they may not teach him Christian doctrine during school. If they could, every Christian parent in America who volunteers in a classroom would be teaching the Bible.

> "Last week, I talked to a Christian lady who is a teacher in a large 'brick and mortar' charter school program in Colorado. She said many Christian families are using the program and enrolling their children in the charter school. I asked her if the teachers could teach the Bible. She said, 'No but we can teach virtues.' I asked if she was allowed to teach the children about salvation and she said, 'We are not supposed to.' If you cannot teach the Bible and the children about Jesus, what is the point of Christian education?"
>
> Attorney Chris Klicka. "Virtual Charter Schools." 10-2001.

Children in charter schools are public school students. Charter schools are funded by taxpayer monies and, according to the California Constitution, all publicly funded schools must be under the "exclusive control of the officers of the public schools." The very heart of homeschooling is the return of that control to the parents. This cannot happen within a charter school.

Non-Christian Philosophy and Goals

Trying to give children a Christian education within a system which does not function from a biblical basis requires a continual shift of perspectives, from secular to Biblical and back again. This creates a double-minded man, who attempts to deal with life sometimes from a biblical perspective and sometimes from a humanist perspective.

If the goal of education is to bring children to a saving knowledge of Jesus Christ, to raise them to glorify God and love the Lord their God with all their heart, mind, soul, and strength ... If the goal is to raise children who know God's Word and are able to apply God's wisdom to every situation they encounter throughout their lives, then an education program is needed which openly declares Christ as Savior and King. This cannot happen within a charter school.

Non-Christian Influences

There is no guarantee that children in charter schools will be assigned a Christian teacher. Charter schools cannot lawfully consider religious affiliation when hiring teachers or other staff. And since charter schools cannot consider religious affiliation when enrolling students, there is also no way of knowing whether the other students participating in various school activities are Christians.

Privately homeschooling parents can ensure that only professing Christians influence their children. They can also maintain full authority over all activities which provide opportunities for others to develop relationships with their children. This cannot happen in a charter school.

> "Home school parents originally fought to be separate from the public schools in order to have the right to choose the curriculum that they believe would be best for their child. Parents removed their children from the public school system because of the non-Christian curriculum. So why would they want to go back to the same humanistic material? But this is happening with homeschoolers who enroll in charter schools or public school programs for home schooling."
>
> Chris Klicka in "Virtual Charter Schools."

Non-Christian Curriculum

Charter schools are prohibited by law from purchasing religious materials, and they are prohibited from allowing religious materials to be used in their programs even if those materials are purchased by parents or others. Parents of any public school student may supplement their children's education with Christian materials, but this must be done outside of regular school time.

In his "Preface to the Holy Bible," Noah Webster wrote, "The Scriptures were intended by God to be the guide of human reason." Biblical teaching is not merely supplemental; rather, it is essential and foundational. Such open recognition of this primary position of Scripture cannot happen in a charter school.

Non-Christian Tests

Beginning with the graduating class of 2004, all public school students, including those in charter schools, must pass the California High School Exit Exam (HSEE) in order to get a high school diploma. The content of the HSEE is dictated by the California State Board of Education and is aligned with the secular content standards for each subject area: "The content standards also serve as the basis for the curriculum frameworks, and all adopted instructional materials and state tests are aligned with them." (California Department of Education. California High School Exit Examination.) The only way to opt out of having government bureaucrats dictate what your student will learn is to opt out of the government tests entirely. But this is not an option in the charter schools.

> "How can schools best prepare students for the HSEE?
>
> It will be important that students take classes that include instruction in state content standards for English/language arts and math. Students will need to use their knowledge of the content identified for the test."
>
> High school exit Examination: Q & A for Teachers.

Non-Christian Control of Your Child's Education

The discerning parent will note that there is a difference between parental involvement and parental control. God has not ordained that parents should have a government facilitator, specialist, guide, teacher, advisor, or assessor for the training of their children to His glory.

It is important for parents to recognize the subtle undermining of the God-ordained family order. Parents are the ones who are responsible for educating their children, not civil government. Roy Hanson, private and home school legislative consultant, stated it well:

> ### Christian Home Education
> - The parents have 100% responsibility
> - The parents have 100% authority

"When we choose not to look to the government, but rather to take full personal responsibility for our children's education, we acknowledge the authority of God and His Word in our lives. We teach our children to honor God, His Word, and His ordained jurisdictions of authority and responsibility. We also teach them to be content with what God provides through our faith and diligent obedient labors." (Roy M. Hanson. "Charter Schools." The Court Report. HSLDA: Jan/Feb 2002.)

Non-Christian Yoking

Charter schools offering independent study require the parents to enter into a contract with the government school:

> "It soon became apparent that the teachers were required to talk to the children at these visits and assess them not only on their academics, but also on their physical appearance ... looking for signs of abuse and/or neglect at their discretion. I had gotten so used to living my own life and had forgotten just how involved the government is in the lives of families enrolled in public schools."
>
> Letter from a home schooling parent to Attorney Chris Klicka. Quoted from "Virtual Charter Schools."

"Each written agreement shall be signed, prior to the commencement of independent study, by the pupil, the pupil's parent, legal guardian, or caregiver, if the pupil is less than 18 years of age, the certificated employee who has been designated as having responsibility for the general supervision of independent study, and all persons who have direct responsibility for providing assistance to the pupil." (California Education Code § 51747 (c)(8))

"Do not be unequally yoked together with unbelievers. For what fellowship has righteousness with lawlessness? And what communion has light with darkness?" 2 Corinthians 6:14

"Blessed is the man who walks not in the counsel of the ungodly. . ." from Psalm 1:1

Non-Christian Funding Methods

Some parents have looked at charter schools as an opportunity to get back some of the hard-earned money they paid in taxes to support public schools. The truth is that when private school students switch to charter schools, it creates an additional tax burden. The best

> "It is also true that your neighbor with no children pays taxes for schools. What is his fair share?"
>
> Ray Stalker. A Response to Parents: Freedom Is the Issue. 2000.

way for families to get the benefit of more of their own money is to work toward reducing government spending.

Parents pay the same amount of taxes whether their children are in a public school, private school, home school, or stay home with a hired tutor. The difference is whether parents add to the tax burden by insisting that they get a piece of the tax fund pie. And when parents consider the incredible spiritual cost to their children's real education by subjecting them to godless government schooling, it's easy to see why it's worth the extra cost of paying for your own children's education.

> To pay enough taxes to cover the ADA funding for two elementary-age children, parents must fit the following example every year:
> Own a home that is assessed for property taxes at a value of $1,500,000, or more *and*
> Spend over $68,000 per year on items which are charged sales tax, *and*
> Have a taxable income of over $90,000 per year.
> "I Want My Money Back." The Parent Educator. Christian Home Educators Press: April/May 2000.

Destruction of Christian Freedom

The charter school movement is a serious threat to true family freedom for several reasons. First, when families participate in charter schools, they support the assumption among many "professionals" that parents are incapable of raising their children without government supervision. Second, as larger numbers of families leave private education in favor of charter schools, it weakens the private education movement by reducing their numbers. Third, as charter school members increasingly earn the reputation of wanting their "share" of taxpayer funds, they become just another special interest group trying to get money, at least in the eyes of the legislature.

Conclusion

The charter school option may look good at first glance. The financial cost of private home education may seem high when compared with the "free" benefits offered by the charter schools. But when parents consider the cost of their children's future, their Christian discipleship, then the truth becomes clear. The financial cost of keeping children away from a system that cannot openly proclaim Christ and His Word is a small price to pay. The Christian education that is necessary to raise children to the glory of God simply cannot be found in a charter school.

This article is available from CHEA as a separate brochure called "Why Charter Schools Won't Work for Christians."

Withdrawing from School

If your children have been in school previously, you must formally withdraw them and enroll them in your private homeschool. Neglecting this important step can lead to truancy investigations, since the school will consider your children absent until they know that your children are enrolled elsewhere. If you follow the procedures described in this section, you can withdraw your child and enroll them into your own homeschool or into a PSP, and no one should question the legitimacy of your actions.

Some families discuss their decision to homeschool with their children's school principal or teachers before they withdraw their children. This is not advisable. Some school staff members are understanding and helpful, but others are hostile and may cause problems. However, if you are in a situation where you feel you must explain why your children will not be returning, call HSLDA first and follow their advice on what to say.

Steps to Take BEFORE Withdrawing Your Children

For the smoothest transition to homeschooling, complete the following steps before you withdraw your children:

1. Read through at least the first two chapters of this book so that you understand the law and your rights, and are prepared to begin homeschooling.

2. Join CHEA of California. As a member, you'll have access to the latest information, plus, you'll receive a substantial discount on your HSLDA membership.

3. Join HSLDA and confirm your membership acceptance.

4. File a private school affidavit (if you are going to set up your own private school) or join a PSP.

When to Withdraw Your Children

Because absences of more than three days generally trigger truancy investigations, you must be sure that your withdrawal is complete before the third consecutive day that your children don't show up for school. By preparing ahead, you can mail the withdrawal on your children's last day of school, so that it will arrive within one or two days, before any truancy issues are raised.

However, if it's possible, the best time to withdraw your children is shortly before the new school year begins, at the end of summer break, when the children have not yet missed any school days at all. For schools following a traditional schedule starting during August or September, this means withdrawing your children in early August, before the first day of public school in your area. Many students withdraw at this time of year, so your withdrawal request will not draw as much attention as it would during the school term. The next best time to avoid attention would be to withdraw your children at the end of Christmas or Easter vacation, or at a semester break.

It is not absolutely necessary to withdraw your children in the fall or at holidays. Children do change schools throughout the year. If your child is having problems at school, it may be better to withdraw him immediately rather than waiting for a natural break in the school calendar.

The Withdrawal Process

There are two parts to the withdrawal process. First is notifying the school that your children will not be returning because they are enrolling in a new school, and second is requesting that the students' records be transferred to the new school. The notification of withdrawal is usually completed by a student's parents, and the request for transfer of records is usually completed by the new school.

If you are beginning your own private school at home rather than joining a PSP, you wear both hats now: you're the student's parent *and* you're the new school administrator. So you can complete both steps at once, following the example shown in the "Withdrawal and Request to Transfer Records" below.

Harborview Christian School
45 N. Elm Street • Anaheim, California 92803 • (714) 555-1234

Withdrawal and Request for Transfer of Records

John Jones, Principal
Olde Public Elementary School
100 Main Street
Anaheim, California, 92803

August 10, 2012

Dear Mr. Jones:

The following children are withdrawing from attendance at Olde Public Elementary School effective on August 10, 2012. They have enrolled in Harborview Christian School. Please forward their school records, including grades and health records.

Student	Grade	Birthdate
Julie Smith	4	8/10/2002
Harold Smith	6	4/18/2000

Thank you.

Arnold Smith

Arnold Smith
School Administrator

Follow this sample, if you have filed your own private school affidavit, to both withdraw your children from school and request their records to be transferred to your new private school. Be sure that the effective date is either the first day of school or the first day your children will be absent from the old school.

If you enroll your children in a PSP, you will perform the first part of withdrawing your children, as the students' parent. Then the PSP administrator will request that the records be transferred to the new school. Below is a sample letter of withdrawal by parent:

Arnold and Carol Smith
45 N. Elm Street
Anaheim, California 92803
(714) 555-1234

August 10, 2012

John Jones, Principal
Olde Public Elementary School
100 Main Street
Anaheim, California, 92803

Dear Mr. Jones:

This is to inform you that as of August 10, 2012, our children, Julie Smith and Harold Smith, are withdrawing from attendance at Olde Public Elementary School. They have enrolled in Harborview Christian School.

[You may want to include a brief paragraph expressing your appreciation for the school and its programs.]

Thank you.

Arnold Smith

Arnold Smith

Use this letter to withdraw your children from their previous school and verify with your PSP that the PSP administrator will send a request for transfer of records.

Whether you send a "withdrawal and request to transfer records" or just a withdrawal, be sure that the effective date is either the first day of the new school year or the first day your children will be absent from the old school. Also, make sure that it arrives before your children have missed three consecutive school days so no truancy investigation will be triggered.

If things go well, as they usually do, this will be the beginning and end of the matter. Once in a while a very conscientious secretary or principal may phone you to ask a few questions. If you have enrolled your child in a private PSP, say that your children have enrolled in a private school and give the name and phone number for the PSP. If they continue to question you, politely explain that they will have to talk to the school administrator for information about the school. If you have established your own private school, and they question you, be ready with your facts and express your plans with confidence. Should someone try to tell you that what you are doing is not legal, simply tell them that your children are now enrolled in a private school.

Occasionally, if the school knows the records are going to a home educating parent, the school will refuse or at least question your right to receive your child's records. However, E.C. § 49069 spells out the "absolute right [of the parent] to access to any and all pupil records related to their children. ... The editing or withholding of any such records . . .. is prohibited." If the school refuses to transfer the students' records, contact HSLDA.

If You Decide to Stop Homeschooling

If you ever decide to stop homeschooling and send your child to public school or a different private school, this process is somewhat reversed.

To enroll your child in the public school system, simply go to the office and register the child. They will send your school a request for your children's records, and you should send the records. You can expedite the process by simply taking a copy of your child's cum file with you. Remember to keep the originals and just give copies to the new school. The child should be placed at his grade level. However, it is quite common for the school to test your child for grade level before placing him.

If your child has completed any part of high school at home, be prepared — the new school is not obligated to honor any credits awarded nor classes completed outside of their school system. While public schools must let your child enroll, he may be entering with no credits, thus starting over at ninth grade. If a private school allows your child to enroll, they may be easier to work with regarding credits already completed, but be sure to ask.

Chapter Two

Establishing a Private School

Setting Up Your Private School

Your school is just like any other private school, even though yours is located in a home and your children are the only enrolled students. If you enroll your children in a PSP, some of the steps will be done by the PSP administrator. If you use an out-of-state program, you will still need to either establish a private school in California or enroll in a California PSP. Whichever alternative you use, the information in this chapter is important to know.

Join CHEA

As a CHEA Member, you'll have access to the latest information, as well as other benefits, including a substantial discount on your HSLDA membership.

Join Home School Legal Defense Association

As soon as you are sure you are going to homeschool, you should apply for membership in HSLDA. While homeschooling *is* legal in California, as well as in every state, there are legal challenges every year. Sometimes a concerned relative or neighbor will report a homeschool family for not sending their children to school, initiating a truancy investigation.

Do not wait to apply to HSLDA after you have already begun homeschooling; you should have your acceptance in hand before withdrawing your children from school. If you have already taken your children out of school, call HSLDA (540-338-5600) to apply using their expedited option. Since HSLDA gives a discount on their membership fee to all CHEA Members, you should join CHEA first, then apply to HSLDA.

Name Your School

You will need to name your school for your dealings with the state. A name is also helpful as you purchase books, arrange field trips, and help your children understand they are not just staying home for fun. Some families even order T-shirts and sweatshirts with their school name and logo to encourage the children to think of their school as real and unique.

Consider carefully the name of your school. A name that is really cute for your primary students can be embarrassing for your older children. Happy Haven Private School sounds adorable for your young children but doesn't look professional on high school transcripts. Some families choose to use the family name, such as Smith Academy. Others use their street name (Maple Street School) or town name (Madera Christian School).

Of course, if you enroll your children in a PSP, it will already have a school name, so you won't choose one.

Private School Affidavit

All private schools are required by the state to file a private school affidavit each year in October. If you enroll in a PSP, you don't need to be concerned about this because the PSP will file the affidavit on behalf of all enrolled students. Step-by-step directions for how to file are included at the end of this chapter.

School Course Of Study

A course of study is the list of subjects offered by a school. California private schools are required to "offer instruction in the several branches of study [i.e., subjects] required to be taught in the public schools." (E.C. §48222) Of course, "offering" instruction may not be the same as "taking" instruction. Thus private schools must offer studies in the subjects on the following list, but each student does not necessarily have to study all of them. For example, some private school students do not study a foreign language even though it is offered by their school.

Additionally, you are free to require additional subjects as you choose. This means that designing your course of study can be as simple as using the list of subjects required to be taught in public schools, or you can customize it to suit your own goals.

Of course, Bible is not one of the government-required subjects, but for Christian homeschoolers, it's the most important one — so important, in fact, that all the other subjects flow from it. It's not enough to just "add" Bible to the list; you should consider the Bible as the foundation of all the subjects on the list, even if you teach a separate Bible course.

The seven state-required subjects for grades 1 to 6:

- English,

- arithmetic,

- social science,

- science,

- fine arts,

- health, and

- P.E.

For junior high and high school (grades 7 to 12) the same subjects are required, plus these four:

- foreign language,

- applied arts,

- career technical education, and

- parenting skills.

Individual Student's Course of Study

Most home educators, like one-room schoolteachers, find it useful to develop an individualized course of study for each student annually and keep it on file. This will help you keep on track toward meeting your educational goals as you progress through the school year.

Your student's course of study may be simply a list of which subjects from the school's course of study will be taught during the school year. Or, you can include more detail about the content you plan to teach each year, to refer to when you make lesson plans.

Your student does not have to study each subject every year. Also, even though a subject appears on your course of study for a particular school year, it does not have to be taught every day. Health, for example, might be taught once or twice a week. You may choose to teach some subjects daily, while teaching others on a rotating schedule. For example, some homeschoolers teach history on Mondays and Wednesdays, then teach science on Tuesdays and Thursdays. Or they teach history in the fall and science in the spring.

You are not required to teach particular subjects in certain grades. In other words, you don't have to follow the public schools' course of study for each grade level. This issue often comes up concerning California History. In most public schools, it is taught in the fourth grade. However, you may choose to teach it sooner or later, depending on the needs of your children or family. The same is true of all subjects.

Content of Courses

Private schools are free to determine their own course content within each branch of study. Also note that studies within these branches of study don't have to be offered as separate courses; they can be combined as you wish. So the homeschool parent chooses content for each school subject. For example, a parent may cover the following specifics for his student's course in English: spelling, homophones and homographs, plurals and possessives, parts of sentences, listening skills, etc. A different parent may choose to cover poetry, punctuation, reading, and vocabulary.

Ideas for topics to include within each subject are found in such documents as *A Typical Course of Study by World Book Encyclopedia* (www.worldbook.com) or in the scope and sequence published by each major curriculum producer for its own curriculum. A scope and sequence tells you what specific areas are covered in each subject in each textbook. Even if you are not using a particular publisher's textbooks, their scope and sequence can be useful for choosing your own study ideas.

It is not necessary, and sometimes not desirable, to strictly adhere to a scope and sequence or typical course of study. These can be helpful as idea sources while you determine what you want to teach your child, but they are not meant to be the dictators of your school's course of study.

Curriculum

Curriculums vary in level of difficulty and teaching styles. You should order several catalogs and see the books if possible. You may visit a local Christian school to see the resources or look through the materials other home educators in your area are using. Some support groups host curriculum fairs where members and publishers' representatives display materials. In many areas of the state there are homeschool curriculum stores with walk-in hours where you can look at the resources. The most complete showing of curriculum is at the Exhibit Hall at the Annual CHEA Convention, featuring more than 200 exhibitors. CHEA also holds the Bay Area Convention in the spring with a good-sized Exhibit Hall.

Post Office Box

If you are setting up your own private school rather than enrolling your children in a PSP, you may want to obtain a post office box. While this is optional, some people prefer to give a post office box number as their school address because it is less obviously a homeschool. This comes in particularly handy with teenaged students who must fill out forms that require both a home and school address, such as when getting a driver's license or work permit.

If you file an affidavit and have six or more children enrolled, your school name will be listed in the *Private School Directory* by the Department of Education, and you will receive lots of mail directed to schools. Some of it will be interesting and helpful, but a lot of it will be junk mail. If you have a post office box, you can sort your mail right over the post office trash receptacles. (Saves bringing more junk mail into your home.)

Stationery

It is highly recommended that you have school letterhead if you are establishing your own private school. You can create a letterhead template on your computer. The stationery can be used on many occasions, making business tasks somewhat easier. It will also give you confidence when you handle school business, giving you a serious, professional appearance.

When you correspond concerning your school, always use your stationery, and keep a copy of all letters for your files. Choose a good, conservative business-sized paper. In addition to the school name and address (be sure to use your post office box if you have chosen this option), some families add a logo.

Using your computer, you can print your own return address on the envelope. You can also purchase or make stick-on return labels. Be sure the envelopes are business-sized and the same color as your stationery.

School Supplies

You can homeschool without a lot of supplies or curriculum. Indeed, families on a budget have successfully homeschooled with only a Bible, library card, and a few worksheets or inexpensive workbooks for arithmetic. Nevertheless, most homeschoolers find it useful to purchase more materials and supplies than this.

Since each family is unique, the supplies that have proven invaluable vary more than you might think. Ask ten different homeschoolers and you will get ten different lists of necessary supplies. Some families say desks for each student are a must; others prefer to work at the kitchen table. Probably the best advice is to start simply, especially when your children are young, adding supplies only as you are certain you will use them.

Most cities have a school supply store. Often they can give you a source for what they do not carry. However, a local source may be more convenient, faster, and cheaper than ordering online after you consider shipping. Stationary stores, bookstores, and discount office supply stores carry many of the items you want. School textbook publishers also frequently carry other supplies.

Of course, you can find many supplies available on the Internet as well.

Supplies for the Homeschool

These supplies are for you as the teacher or are the sort of thing students can share. Some items, such as a good dictionary, are essential for all homeschools. Other items, such as a microscope, could be essential if you're studying a particular subject. Finally, lots of these things are just in the category of "nice to have." For example, a copier is very handy, but you can certainly homeschool successfully without one.

1. Each student needs a personal Bible

2. Concordance and other Bible study aids

3. Dictionary (Webster's 1828 Dictionary is highly recommended, particularly for the teacher and older students.)

4. Basic reference books: encyclopedia set, atlas, thesaurus, etc.

5. Wall map or globe

6. Art supplies: paper, paint, paint brushes, glue, finger paints, etc.

7. Equipment for experiments: microscope, magnifying glass, magnets, prisms, bug box, etc.

8. Math manipulatives (These can be purchased at a school supply store. Legos®, beans, and other items around the home can be used as well.)

9. Audio/video equipment: CD player and recorder, DVD player, MP3 player

10. Computer and printer, with Internet access

11. Home copier (one that can enlarge is handy)

12. White board, chalk board, felt board, bulletin board

13. Games and puzzles

14. Library of reading books: storybooks for young children, classics for older ones.

15. Book shelf for that growing library

16. Office supplies: stapler, staples, and staple remover, 3-hole punch, paper clips, etc. Remember, in addition to

teaching your children, you're now running a school office.

17. Notebook for lesson plans

18. File box or file cabinet for school records

Supplies for Each Student

These things need to be considered separately for each student. While students could certainly share a ruler and eraser, most homeschool moms have found that a separate school box for each child avoids waiting and arguments, and helps to teach children responsibility and organization. Again, what your own children need will depend on their ages and the subjects you're studying each year.

As Christian home educators, everything we teach is from a biblical foundation. For that reason, it is important to have a good study Bible for each child.

Additionally, consider the following:

1. Desk and chair (Many homeschoolers prefer the kitchen table instead.)

2. Paper, both lined and blank

3. A school supply box with pencils, pens, crayons, markers, eraser, scissors, ruler, compass, protractor

4. Notebook for each child

As you look through catalogs or stroll through an exhibit hall, you will see many teaching aids that will excite you. You can have an elaborate or a simple "school room," or none at all. Please remember this list of supplies is only a recommendation and is intended to help you think through what you need. You certainly don't need it all. Set a budget when you begin homeschooling and choose just what you need to get started. Over the years your library and supply shelf will grow.

Private School Requirements

Parents have been legally conducting their own private schools in their homes for many years. Neither the State Department of Education nor any county or local public school districts have jurisdiction over the establishment or operation of private elementary and secondary schools. All legal requirements are set forth in the California Education Code. But before we look at those requirements, consider a few items that are *not required*:

Items that Are NOT Required

Size of School

There are no requirements relating to the number of pupils or teachers in a school. Thus a school can range from having just one pupil to thousands and can have just one teacher, a couple of part-time teachers, or as many teachers as are needed.

School Building

There is no requirement that schools must have a particular type of building, although schools which have more than 50 students or more than one classroom must meet certain safety requirements. So your children's school can be in your home.

School Equipment and Supplies

There are no requirements related to school equipment such as desks, chalkboards, number of books, etc. Each school is free to determine what equipment is used in its programs.

Number of School Days

Private schools are not required to operate the same number of days per year (currently 175-180) as public schools. However, even though there is no required number of days, if your children don't attend a "full-time" private day school, they may be charged with truancy. Worse yet, they may be uneducated. With no specific requirements for school days, you have great flexibility in planning your school schedule; however, a good goal would be to aim for around 175 days per school year.

Remember that even in the public schools, pupils and teachers often miss days for illness or other excused reasons. These excused absences count in the days of attendance, so if you or your child are sick during the school year, you don't need to make up those missed days during the summer.

Number of Hours

There is no required number of hours per school day for private schools. Public schools must operate a minimum of three hours and twenty minutes for grades 1-3, and four hours for grades 4-12; however, there are multiple exceptions which allow for shorter minimum days.

While these requirements do not apply to private schools, it is probably wisest to plan for around three hours for the lower grades and four for the upper grades. Remember, though, that home economics, independent study time, reading, discussion time, field trips, and activities can all be included in school time.

Tests

There are no requirements for private school students to take tests of any sort — no standardized exams, no High School Exit Exam, no final exams for courses, no exams at all. This means it is entirely up to you, as the private school administrator and teacher, whether to have your student take tests, as well as when to take them and what type of test to use.

What *Is* Required?

Most requirements for private schools are set forth in E.C. §§ 48222 and 33190. The same requirements apply to all private schools regardless of whether they are campus-based or home-based. Here are the basic requirements:

Full-time Private Day School

While there are no specific requirements as to number of days or hours, your private school does have to operate "full time" and offer at least some instruction during the daytime.

Instructors Who Are "Capable of Teaching"

There is no definition of "capable of teaching" and no requirement for a private school teacher to hold a state teaching credential or to have equivalent training. Thus, it is the private school administrators who determine if teachers in the school are capable of teaching.

Teacher Qualifications

The names and addresses, including city and street, of its faculty, together with a record of the educational qualifications of each teacher must be kept on file.

In preparing a document that outlines your qualifications as a teacher, you should begin to

> # E.C. § 48222. Attendance in Private School
>
> Children who are being instructed in a private full-time day school by persons capable of teaching shall be exempted. Such school shall, except under the circumstances described in Section 30, be taught in the English language and shall offer instruction in the several branches of study required to be taught in the public schools of the state. The attendance of the pupils shall be kept by private school authorities in a register, and the record of attendance shall indicate clearly every absence of the pupil from school for a half day or more during each day that school is maintained during the year.
>
> Exemptions under this section shall be valid only after verification by the attendance supervisor of the district, or other person designated by the board of education, that the private school has complied with the provisions of Section 33190 requiring the annual filing by the owner or other head of a private school of an affidavit or statement of prescribed information with the Superintendent of Public Instruction. The verification required by this section shall not be construed as an evaluation, recognition, approval, or endorsement of any private school or course.

think of yourself as an educator. The number one qualification is the fact that you are the parent. If you are a credentialed teacher, include that information, but do not be intimidated if you are not a state certified teacher.

Nearly all parents are capable to teach their own children. Be creative, but be honest. Put down any schooling, high school graduation and above. Include work experience, skills, hobbies, interests, and any personal information that adds to your qualifications to teach such as a love of traveling and adventure, an inquiring mind, or love of reading, etc. Other qualifications can be leader of youth organization, church school teacher, and attendance at educational conferences. CHEA of California holds such conferences twice a year. (Schools call this In-Service Training.)

English Instruction

Instruction must be taught in English, but there is an exception provided in E.C. § 30: "... any private school may determine when and under what circumstances instruction may be given bilingually." That section of the Education Code goes on to state:

> It is the policy of the state to insure the mastery of English by all pupils in the schools; provided that bilingual instruction may be offered in those situations when such instruction is educationally advantageous to the pupils. Bilingual instruction is authorized to the extent that it does not interfere with the systematic, sequential, and regular instruction of all pupils in the English language.

Based on that code section, the general rule for non-English-speaking families seems to be that if the parents or child do not speak English, the private school instruction may be in the family's native language. However, there must be a goal of bringing the student to proficiency in English.

Based on this requirement, families can learn English together as part of their regular course of study. In other words, it would be appropriate for the family to use materials for most subjects in the language they speak, and then to use a program for learning English as a separate class until the English language is mastered.

Course of Study

The courses of study offered by the institution must be kept on file. This could be as simple as just a list of the required subjects.

Branches of Study

Instruction must be offered "in the several branches of study required to be taught in the public schools." For grades 1-6, the required branches of study are English, mathematics, social sciences, science, visual and performing arts, health, and physical education. For grades 7-12, the required branches are the same as those for grades 1-6, plus foreign language, applied arts, and career-technical education. Parenting skills must also be taught in grades 6-9, but this topic is often included as part of another course, for example, social studies. Driver education is now optional for private schools but may be taught if desired.

Attendance Records

Attendance records of each enrolled student must be kept in a register indicating every absence of a half-day or more.

Verification and the Private School Affidavit

A Private School Affidavit must be filed by the school's administrator with the California Superintendent of Public Instruction between October 1 and 15 of each year. The attendance supervisor for the local school district has the authority to verify that an affidavit has been filed, but this is rarely an issue because once filed, the affidavit is a public record. Typically the local districts have access to the affidavits online and won't need to call you at all. If you are called, you can simply offer to send a copy of the affidavit along with the confirmation page showing it was filed.

Health Records

There are several required health records your school must keep. Because these can be confusing, each is explained individually in the section "Required Health Records."

Records to Keep

It is very important to keep accurate records of what you are doing. Your records will help keep you organized and aware of your children's progress. They will also be verification of your validity as a private school should you ever be questioned. You want to be taken seriously, not only for your own sake but for the sake of the entire homeschooling movement, so set up your school as professionally as possible and teach with a professional attitude. Remember, you are an educator.

Another reason your records will be important is in case you ever decide to return your children to the public or private school system or they ever need a transcript for work, college, military service, or insurance.

There are some items that private schools must, by law, keep in their files. Other items are optional.

You can keep your files in whatever fashion you desire as long as they are neat, orderly, and easily accessible. You can use a three-ring binder, file folder, or official-looking printed cumulative folder for your child's records. Digital recording systems are also available.

If possible, correspondence and records should be typed using good quality, business-sized paper. Keep copies of all official correspondence to or from anyone concerning your school.

Records Required by Law

These are the records that are legally required to be kept by private schools, whether PSPs enrolling students from many families or private schools consisting of just one family:

1. Attendance record or register for each child (E.C. § 48222).

2. Course of study offered by the school (E.C. § 33190).

3. The name, address, and educational qualifications of each member of the faculty, which is you (E.C. § 33190).

4. Criminal record summary of all employees, other than parents working exclusively with their own children (E.C. §§ 33190 and 44237). Note that nearly all home-schools are exempt from this requirement because parents are teaching their own children. Any other teachers that you use could fit within this requirement if they are paid employees.

5. Immunization records or waiver (HSC §§ 120325-120375.)

6. Report of Health Examination for School Entry or waiver of Health Check-Up for School Entry (within 90 days of entering first grade) (HSC § 12040).

Because the Private School Affidavit is required to by filed by private schools, you should also keep a copy of it in your files.

Since these records are required of *schools*, you are only required to have them if you establish your own private school. If your children are enrolled in a PSP, the PSP keeps these records. However, even if your children are enrolled in a PSP, it is recommended that you retain copies of these documents for your own records.

Other Records You Should Keep

In addition to the required records already listed, there are other common records that you should keep. These are listed separately because they are recommendations, not legal requirements.

There are three basic types: (1) school records, (2) teaching records, and (3) individual pupil records (called cumulative or "cum" files). Each of the three types will be discussed in turn, but you can see why they may be confusing to homeschoolers: *you* run a school, so you now keep school records; *you* are the teacher, so you will begin to accumulate teaching records; and your children are the students, so their cum files will be your responsibility as the school administrator! Thus, it's easy to mix the records together in your file cabinet. (But we hope you won't do that.)

If you run your own private school (filing your own affidavit) you will want to have one file folder for school records and a separate cum file folder for each child. Teaching records should be kept separately in another file folder or in a teacher's notebook.

School Records

Most of the school records you need are required by law and were discussed in the previous section. Since they are school records, the attendance logs, course of study, and faculty qualifications all should be kept in a "school file." All these are private records belonging to your school that you only need show by order of a court. Since a court order is unlikely, what this means is these records, while required, are yours if you're the school's owner.

Additionally, there are two more items which, while not required by law, should be kept in your "school file." First, as already mentioned, keep a copy of your private school affidavit. Second, although it is not required by law, keep a copy of your school's philosophy, as described in chapter one.

Teaching Records

Also known as educational or daily records, teaching records include daily lesson plans, unit study outlines, field trip journals, reading lists, and samples of student work, which are all commonly kept by teachers. These items are valuable aids for planning next year's lessons, helping keep to one's goals, and showing a student's progress. (Kids love to look at reports they wrote when they were small.)

There is no legal requirement for teachers to keep teaching records at all, but homeschoolers should save them as long as they would be useful in court, will help with planning lessons for younger children, or have sentimental value. HSLDA recommends that homeschooling parents keep such records in case they are ever called to account because of home instruction. It is not necessary, however, to keep every paper or project your children do.

For younger children who are not in formal academics (perhaps under ages eight to ten), you may want to use a notebook, diary, or journal to chronologically list your everyday activities. These entries would focus on the educational knowledge derived from the activities and experiences. For instance, you would list books you read to the children, field trips, sports activities, what your children learned while cooking, sewing, gardening, building together, etc.

You should keep a file of special artwork and writings by your child. At this age you may not want them to do an abundance of papers or workbooks, but most children will do some of this type of work. So you may want to keep those papers.

For children in formal academics, you may want to give each child a notebook or folder. A page for each subject could be included listing each book as your child finishes it, or you may list all the books in the curriculum and check them off as you go along. Your child may complete as many books and grade levels during the school year as he desires, working at his individual pace. Your child will also enjoy picking out special papers or reports to place in his notebook.

Besides the basic subjects, you should keep track of extra-curricular activities. Make note of classes taken through other organizations, such as driver's education and training, swimming, gymnastics, speed-reading, or computer programming. Include work programs, job training, apprenticeships, 4-H projects, and so on. Note other skills such as sewing, animal husbandry, cooking, or car maintenance.

Keep a list of books read by each child. As this list grows, it is a source of encouragement to your child and an important record of achievements. You may want to use a blank Bible study diary or a devotional diary for this purpose.

You may want to provide each child with an assignment book or sheets on which you have written what is expected for the day or week. The assignment book could be separate, or the sheets could be kept in the notebook with completed assignments. At the end of the year file the assignment records and schoolwork away. This information can also be kept in computer files or written in journal form.

After a year or two, you may want to pare down what you have kept and continue to only keep a representation of this work. That way you will always have proof of your student's progress, but without bulging filing cabinets. A good way to do this is, at the end of each school year, have your children sift through all of their papers and take out those that they want to keep. These papers can then be taken to a quick print shop and bound. For big projects, like the sugar cube mission or a biology dissection, take photographs and place them in an album. Have your children write their own comments about the pictures and include any written reports.

Individual Pupil Records (Cum Files)

Individual Pupil Records are called "cum files," since they are a cumulative record of a pupil's school experience. The California Education Code and the California Administrative Code set requirements for individual pupil records that must be maintained by public schools.

While there is some disagreement about what records private schools are required to keep, it makes sense to keep cum files in a format that the receiving school will understand if your student ever transfers. If your student will never attend public schools, you won't need to spend too much time worrying about whether the records conform to the public school's. Even if a decision is later made to send the child to a public or private campus day school, it is not too difficult to translate the years of homeschooling into understandable pupil records if you have kept good teaching records.

However, since it is best to be prepared for the unexpected, and since cum files are easy to maintain, it's recommended that you have a cum file for each of your students.

If your children are enrolled in a PSP, the PSP will keep a cum file. But you ought to keep one yourself, too. Since you are ultimately responsible for your children's education, it is important that you also take the ultimate responsibility for keeping and maintaining their records. And occasionally a PSP has closed or changed staff on short notice, making it difficult if not impossible to obtain students' records.

Therefore, make copies of all your children's records before giving any originals to your PSP. Also, if you transfer your students to a new school, make copies and send those, keeping the originals in your own permanent file.

You can buy specially printed cum file folders from a school supplier. These manila file folders have a printed section to record subjects, course titles, grades, and credits. This section could be photocopied to use as a transcript for college admissions. Some cum file folders include space for optional information like test scores, special interests and activities, and teacher's comments.

Most cum file folders have spaces for much more information than is necessary. (For example, A Beka's has a place for economic status of the family.) Don't feel that you have to fill out every blank. Just adapt the forms to suit your needs. Or you can simply use a plain manila folder to keep each student's records together.

Permanent Pupil Records to include in the cum file

To have the cum file resemble a file which a traditional school may use, the following items should be included.

1. Legal name of pupil.

2. Date of birth.

3. Method of verification of birth date.

4. Sex of pupil.

5. Place of birth.

6. Name & address of parent of minor pupil.
   a. Address of minor pupil if different than the above.
   b. An annual verification of the name and address of the parent and the residence of the pupil.

7. Entering and leaving date of each school year and for any summer session or other extra session.

8. Subjects taken during each year, half-year, summer session, or quarter.

9. If marks or credits are given, the mark or number of credits toward graduation.

10. Verification of or exemption from required immunizations.

11. Date of high school graduation or equivalent.

12. The required health records.

You may also want to keep the results of standardized tests in the cum file, but this is not necessary.

Transferring Records

If your student transfers to a new school from your own homeschool, send only individual pupil records (cum files). If your student has been enrolled in a PSP and is transferring, the PSP administrator will transfer their copy of the cum file for you. However, since cum files are private records, the PSP will probably want a written authorization from you before they will send them. The PSP may have their own record transfer request form for you to fill out. If not, you should send a written request to the PSP office. Make sure the request includes where and when you want the records to be sent.

When you transfer records, do not send school records, teaching records, handwritten letters of evaluation, samples of student work, or any other items not listed as part of an individual pupil record.

If a student transfers from a public school into your own private school in your home, "a copy of the pupil's Mandatory Permanent Pupil Record shall be transferred upon request from the . . . private school." (California Administrative Code Title 5-438) The public school will permanently keep either the original or a copy of the Mandatory Permanent Pupil Record.

Required Health Records

There are two categories of Health and Safety Code (HSC) regulations concerning all schools in California, whether public or private.

First are individual health records which must be kept for each student, either in his cum file or in a separate health file. These must be transferred with the student to any new school. The Department of Health has authority to inspect these health records, but other pupil information is confidential.

Second are school health reports that the Health Department sends to some private schools each year. If received, the private school is required to complete the form and return it to the Health Department.

Individual Health Records

There are two individual health records required for each student. It is rare for the Department of Health to ask homeschoolers to inspect these, but they can. Each year a few PSPs are asked to show individual health records, usually because the Department is compiling statistics to assess how well they are doing at encouraging parents to have their children immunized. If you receive a request to show these records, review "Health Department Reviews of Immunization Records" in the section on school health reports.

California School Immunization Record (Form PM286)

All children under 18 years old entering a California public or private school for the first time, or transferring between schools, must present a written immunization record. This immunization record (PM286) must be filed twice, once before entering first grade and again before entering seventh grade. The form is traditionally printed on light blue card stock and so is often referred to simply as the "blue card." You can obtain printed copies from your local health department or you can download it online at www.cdph.ca.gov/pubsforms/forms/CtrldForms/cdph286.pdf.

The immunization record must either be filled out, including the month and year that each vaccine dose was received, or the student may be exempted. Two exemptions are available: a doctor's written exemption for medical reasons or the parents' exemption because of personal beliefs. The parents' exemption may be temporary or permanent, may apply to any or all vaccines, and is made by signing the proper space on the back of the form.

Beginning January 1, 2014 another form is required for an exemption. To waive the mandatory immunizations, another form, "Personal Beliefs Exemption to Required Immunizations" (CDPH-8262) is needed.

Before entering first grade, take the CDPH-8262 to your health care provider medical doctor (M.D.), doctor of osteopathic medicine (D.O.), nurse practitioner, physician assistant, naturopathic doctor, or credentialed school nurse). You may be required to have a discussion about immunizations, attend a formal class about immunizations, or watch a DVD.

Once the provider thinks you have been adequately informed of the consequences of not immunizing your child, the health care provider will fill out and sign the CDHP-8262 certifying the information has been provided. You fill out the rest of the form and then file it with the Immunization Record.

IMPORTANT NOTE: Many health care providers now use an online health care providing program titled CAIR (California Immunization Registry). We do NOT recommend you use this program. All of your child's specific information will be in a public on-line repository. Homeschoolers are private Christian schools at home with the private being essential. This means that the health care provider you visit will need to be sympathetic to your desire for privacy and avoid entering the information into CAIR for you.

Before entering seventh grade, your blue card (PM286B) is required to be updated. Children must receive a Tdap or Adacel or Boostrix immunization on or after their seventh birthday. (It is actually best for the shots to be given closer to your child's tenth birthday so that it will last until high school is finished. The shots are usually effective for about 10 years.) The blue card (PM286B) does not have a space for this immunization. Instead you must contact your local county health department and request the Tdap (Pertussis Booster) Requirement (PM286S) sticker for your child.

It is probably best to do this in a group with other homeschoolers. Your local support group or PSP may join together to call and request a larger number of stickers from the local health department. This way you do not stand out to the health department employee by asking for a single sticker.

Waiving the Tdap Immunization requirement will necessitate you visit your health care provider again. You must print up a fresh blue card (PM286B) and re-sign and re-date the back. You will also need to print up a new copy of CDPH-8262 and listen again to the training your health care provider gives you about waiving your child's immunization. Your provider will fill out the Authorized Health Care Practitioner portion of this form and you will again fill out the parent portions.

You will file this second copy of CDPH-8262 in your child's permanent school record. You should also obtain the PM286S sticker for the front of your blue card. Affix it to the upper left hand corner and check the third box which says: "Tdap personal belief exemption affidavit from parent/guardian on file" and fill out the information on the bottom of the sticker also.

Unless exempted, immunizations are required for the following diseases: diphtheria, hepatitis B, haemophilus influenzae type B, measles, mumps, pertussis (whooping cough), polio¬myelitis, rubella, tetanus and varicella (chickenpox). Mumps and pertussis immunizations are not required for children seven years or older. Some counties also require a tuberculosis skin test for students entering school at specific grade levels.

Contact your doctor or local county health department for more specific information on requirements relating to the number of doses and age requirements. Either the immunization record or the exemption must be on file within 30 days of the beginning of first grade or within 30 days of enrollment of any other grade level student. This record is sent to a new school if the student ever transfers.

Report of Health Exam for School Entry (PM171A) or Waiver (PM171B)

The second required individual health record is the record of health examination for each child prior to entry into school. Students may either be examined by a doctor before entering school, or their parents may waive the examination requirement.

Either the "Report of Health Exam for School Entry" (Form PM171A) or the "Waiver of Health Check-up for School Entry" (Form PM171B) must be kept for each student. Download blank copies on the web. For the PM171A (exam form) go to www. dhcs.ca.gov/formsandpubs/forms/Forms/ChildMedSvcForms/ pm171a(bi).pdf. For the waiver form, go to www.dhcs.ca.gov/ formsandpubs/forms/Forms/ChildMedSvcForms/pm171b(bi). pdf.

Again, this record is to be kept on file for each student and must be sent to a new school if the child transfers.

School Health Reports

If the following reports from the Health Department are received by a school, including a private homeschool, they are legally required to be completed and returned. For any of these reports, send in only the actual report form; do not send in any worksheets or names of students. Any worksheets sent to you are only for your use in preparing the form. Also, you are only required to file these reports if one is sent to you. If you don't receive one, you don't need to file one.

Annual Seventh Grade Immunization Report

Each student entering seventh grade is required to have either a hepatitis B vaccination or a documented waiver stating that the immunization is contrary to personal beliefs. Private school administrators (including private homeschools) could receive a letter from California's Department of Health Services (DHS) requesting that the administrator complete a form to report on the immunization status of all seventh grade students in their schools. The information requested by DHS is the total number of students entering seventh grade and a tally of those students who have had the required immunizations, are exempt based on medical reasons or on personal beliefs, or who have neither had immunizations nor signed exemption waivers and therefore need further follow-up. If you receive this report, make every effort to have no students reported as needing a follow-up on their vaccinations.

Immunization Assessment of Kindergarten Students (Form PM236)

Schools that enroll students in kindergarten are required by state law to submit a completed school Summary Sheet (Form PM236) of the annual "Immunization Assessment of Kindergarten Students" by October 20th of each year. If you receive this form in the mail from the State Department of Health Services and if your private school affidavit indicates that you have enrolled kindergarten students, then complete and send in the PM236 form, including only a tally of the number of immunization verifications.

Since kindergarten is not compulsory, the recommendation is that you avoid dealing with the PM236 report by waiting until your child is six years old and enrolling him directly into the first grade. If you do not have kindergartners listed on your private school affidavit, then you do not have to complete report Form PM236.

Child Health and Disability Prevention (CHDP) Program Report

Every private school which is sent a CHDP program report form is required to complete the form and return it by January 15. Information requested on the form includes the total number of children enrolled in first grade and the number of children who have had a health screening examination or who have a signed waiver. If you have no first graders enrolled, indicate on the form that you have no first graders.

Health Department Reviews of Immunization Records

As explained in the section on individual health records, the State Department of Health Services audits some schools each year to review immunization records. These audits are typically handled through the county health departments. Schools are chosen randomly to provide a sampling of the population, by which the department of health services can determine the success of its immunization programs and determine the need for future programs.

As far as we are aware, some PSPs with many students have been audited by the Department of Health Services, but we know of no single-family homeschools who have been audited. However, there is nothing in the law that would preclude the auditing of smaller schools.

If your county health department notifies you that they want to inspect your students' health records, ask if you may bring the records in for an appointment at the county office. Bring only the immunization records with you, leaving the students' other records at home. Ask the official to review them while you wait, rather than leaving the records with him. If you cannot bring the records to the health department, prepare ahead of time for their appointment at your school by having the health records out, separate from all other individual pupil records, which are private.

If you are a member of HSLDA, call them before you set up an appointment to see if there are any new recommendations. Sometimes PSP administrators have been able to redact some of the identifying information, but usually the department will want to see surnames (for ethnicity identification purposes), birth dates, and dates of exams or immunizations. Some PSP administrators have also been able to arrange to mail in the needed information.

Filing a Private School Affidavit

Because the procedure for filing the annual Private School Affidavit (PSA) may change after the publication date for this manual, please check the CHEA website just prior to filing to see if there are any updates. Go to www.cheaofca.org and click on "Getting Started" to find current PSA information.

What Filing the Affidavit Does

The Education Code requires private schools to file an affidavit each year, but it is important to understand that filing the form does not create a school. If that seems confusing, think of it like you would think of your car: renewing your car's registration each year does not make it a car. Even registering a brand new car for the first time does not make it a car. Registering is simply a legal requirement with which owners of cars must comply. In the same way, filing the affidavit is simply a registration requirement for schools; it has nothing to do with *creating* a private school.

Additionally, filing the affidavit does not mean any official recognition or approval is given to your school by the government; nor does it mean your school is accredited. Filing the affidavit simply means your school has complied with E.C. § 33190, which requires the annual filing.

Where to Go for Help

Do not call public school officials for information on private home education nor on filing a private school affidavit (PSA). Because the public school officials of necessity specialize in public schools, they typically do not understand the law as it relates to private education. Confusing or inaccurate information has been given to private home educators who have contacted the California Department of Education, County Board of Education, or local public school officials. Instead, if you have questions after

E.C. § 33190

Every person, firm , association, partnership, or corporation offering or conducting private school instruction of the elementary or high school level shall between the first and 15th day of October of each year, commencing on October 1, 1967, file with the Superintendent of Public Instruction an affidavit or statement, under penalty of perjury, by the owner or other head setting forth the following information for the current year:

(a) All names, whether real or fictitious, of the person, firm, association, partnership, or corporation under which it has done and is doing business.

(b) The address, including city and street, of every place of doing business of the person, firm, association, partnership, or corporation within the State of California.

(c) The address, including city and street, of the location of the records of the person, firm, association, partnership, or corporation, and the name and address, including city and street, of the custodian of such records.

(d) The names and addresses, including city and street, of the directors, if any, and principal officers of the person, firm, association, partnership, or corporation.

(e) The school enrollment, by grades, number of teachers, coeducational or enrollment limited to boys or girls and boarding facilities.

(f) That the following records are maintained at the address stated, and are true and accurate:

(1) The records required to be kept by Section 48222.

(2) The courses of study offered by the institution.

(3) The names and addresses, including city and street, of its faculty, together with a record of the educational qualifications of each.

(g) Criminal record summary information has been obtained pursuant to Section 44237.

Whenever two or more private schools are under the effective control or supervision of a single administrative unit, such administrative unit may comply with the provisions of this section on behalf of each of the schools under its control or supervision by submitting one report.

Filing pursuant to this section shall not be interpreted to mean, and it shall be unlawful for any school to expressly or impliedly represent by any means whatsoever, that the State of California, the Superintendent of Public Instruction, the State Board of Education, the State Department of Education, or any division or bureau of the department, or any accrediting agency has made any evaluation, recognition, approval, or endorsement of the school or course unless this is an actual fact.

The Superintendent of Public Instruction shall prepare and publish a list of private elementary and high schools to include the name and address of the school and the name of the school owner or administrator.

reading this manual and checking the CHEA website for updates, contact HSLDA.

Who should file a PSA?

Only private schools file PSAs. And only one PSA is filed for each school. So if you're running your own private school in order to homeschool your children, you should file.

Additionally, only children between ages six and 18 are required to attend school. So file only if you have students between those ages. If your oldest child is four or five and you're teaching kindergarten or pre-kindergarten, you don't need to file yet — unless your oldest child will be turning six before September 1.

If you are joining a PSP do not file your own affidavit. You are enrolling your children in an existing private school, and the administrator should file the affidavit each year.

If you are homeschooling under the tutorial exemption because you are a credentialed teacher or have hired one, you do not need to file a PSA. However, many who are qualified to use the tutorial exemption choose to establish a private school in their home and use that exemption instead because the hours and days requirements are more flexible for private schools than for tutors. So you are free to make the choice of which exemption to use if you are qualified for both. If you choose to operate as a

To File Or Not To File

Whether or not to file a Private School Affidavit can be a subject of disagreement. Christians who choose not to file at all typically make one of two arguments: some argue that the state has no authority to demand they register their school with the state; others argue that they have the right to homeschool without being a private school at all.

Christians who do file the PSA typically believe either that not registering is biblical disobedience to the governing authorities, or that filing the PSA is a simple matter that does not restrain their right to homeschool.

Some are concerned that if they do file, the state will have all the information it needs on the PSA to find and possibly harass them. Others think that if they do not file, things will be harder for them if they are ever investigated.

It may help to remember that the affidavit is not an application requiring approval, but is only a statistical tool. The State of California does not accredit schools; neither public nor private. Further, under California law, children must attend public school unless they are exempt. This means that children who are homeschooled without meeting one of the California exemptions are considered truant by California's government officials. So families who don't file the PSA could be charged with truancy and, since they would be in violation of California law, they would need to support their position by arguing the California law is invalid under the U.S. Constitution.

Each family must follow its conscience on this issue.

tutor, don't file; if you choose to operate as a private school, then do file.

If your children are enrolled in a charter school or other public school program, do not file the PSA. Your children are public school students and are thereby in compliance with the compulsory education law — so you don't need an exemption.

When to File the PSA

E.C. § 33190 requires that every private school file a private school affidavit with the Superintendent of Public Instruction at the California Department of Education between October 1 and 15 of each year. If you are setting up your school after October 15 and the private school affidavit is still available online, we recommend that you go ahead and file regardless of the time of year.

How to File the PSA

Before you can fill out the PSA form, you will have to choose a name for your school and designate at least one administrator, who may also be the teacher. In homeschools, it's common for the father to be the principal and teacher, and for the mother to be the administrator and teacher.

The PSA is available online at the California Department of Education (CDE) website: www.cde.ca.gov/sp/ps/rq. Only information required by E. C. 33190 must be included on the affidavit. However, the computerized online affidavit form has been programmed by the CDE to ask for some additional information. When filing online, we recommend that you provide only the asterisked information, which is what is necessary to file your affidavit online.

Because the PSA form requests non-required information, some private schools chose to file their affidavit with a paper form or a "Letter in Lieu." A paper PSA may be requested by calling the CDE at 916-319-0839 or send an e-mail to privateschools@cde. ca.gov."

Finding the Proper PSA Form Online

Currently the CDE has one PSA form for schools with five or fewer students and another for schools with six or more students. The forms are basically the same; the difference is in how the information is processed in the CDE computer system. The larger schools are included in the Private School Directory and are assigned a CDS code number, while the smaller ones are not. Additionally, the larger schools are each given a password when they first file an affidavit. This password allows you access to the form for your school each year. The smaller schools (five or fewer students) do not have

> ## The CDE's "Frequently Asked Questions"
>
> The CDE website includes a section of "Frequently Asked Questions" (FAQ). Their information on homeschooling changes every year or so. The current information is generally not as scary or intimidating as it used to be, but there are still some troubling sections.
>
> For example, one question and answer suggest it's a good idea to call your local school district and announce that you plan to home-school. Don't do that. It's not required and is more likely to raise questions and create problems than to help.
>
> Another question and answer indicate that the local attendance supervisor can have a look at your records any time he or she wants. That's not accurate either. The authority is limited to verifying that the affidavit is filed. Unless someone has a court order or warrant, you don't need to show your records. If someone ever insists that you show your records, call HSLDA.

a password and need to fill out the affidavit form fresh each year following the directions below.

To find the forms, begin at the CDE website for private schools: www.cde.ca.gov/sp/ps/rq. Once there, click on "Filing the Private School Affidavit." Scroll down to where it says, "Filing the Online Affidavit Form" and, below the CDE statement, select the category which best characterizes your private school for filing the affidavit:

1. Existing schools with six or more students (password required)

2. All other schools (blank form)

3. If you have five or fewer students, then select "Schools with five or fewer students."

If your school is in the first category, as explained above, you'll need to enter a password to get to your form. The CDE sends the passwords to the larger schools which filed last year. You should have received it prior to October 1.

If your school is in the second category, a Private School Affidavit Form should appear on the next screen.

Letter in Lieu of the Affidavit Form

The CDE prefers online filing of the Private School Affidavit. When this is not possible, one alternative for filing PSA is a "Letter in Lieu.".

The letter must include all the information required in E.C. § 33190. Additionally, the CDE requires the letter to include the following certification wording: "To the best of my knowledge and belief, the information contained in this Private School Affidavit is true and accurate, and this school is in compliance with E.C. § 44237 to the extent it applies." In addition, the owner or other head of the private school must sign the statement under "penalty of perjury."

Mail the letter via certified mail to:

Title II Leadership - Private Schools
California Department of Education
1430 N St., Ste 4309
Sacramento, CA 95814

Before mailing the letter, make a copy for your file. Also keep the certified mail receipt as proof of mailing. The CDE does not acknowledge receipt of the letter. Therefore, your certified mailing receipt will be your only proof of mailing.

Because the required information is the same whether you use the online PSA form or a letter in lieu, using the online PSA form is recommended. Since most schools use the form, doing so will usually attract less attention than sending a letter.

If your school is in either the second or third category, a Private School Affidavit Form should appear on the next screen. Make sure the date under the form's title indicates the actual school year for which you are filing. If you are attempting to file prior to October 1, it is possible that the form has not yet been updated and you should wait until the current school year's affidavit is available before filing.

Step-By-Step Directions for Filling in the PSA Form

You must complete the form all in one online session; there is no way to save part of it and finish later. An asterisk next to any field on the CDE's online form indicates that the information is required in order to submit your affidavit online.

Fill out the form following these guidelines:

Introductory Information and "Notice"

The paragraph at the top of the form and the "Notice" are for information only. The form begins with the following:

From E.C. § 48222: This is "...a private full-time ... school ... [that] ... offer[s] instruction in the several branches of study required to be taught in public schools of the state ... [that offers this] instruction ... in English [, and that keeps] ... attendance [records ..." *	☐ A Private School Affidavit cannot be filed if the answer to this question is NO.

This is a recitation of the law as covered in previous chapters. You must check "Yes."

School Information

1. Name of School *

Choose a name for your school, if you have not already done so, and enter it here.

2. Enter your CDE-assigned 14 digit CDS code if one was previously assigned.

If you have one, enter it. If you aren't sure, you probably don't, so just leave this blank. See the sidebar on page 90 for more information on CDS codes.

3. County in which school is located. *

Select your county from the pull-down menu.

4. Public school district in which school is located *

If you know the name of the school district in which your private home-based school is located, select it from the pull-down menu. If you live in two districts (i.e. one elementary school district and a different high school district) then select the name of the district that most closely matches the ages and grades of your children. If you live in two districts and your children's ages span all levels, it probably doesn't matter which of the districts you select. If you don't know what district you are in, you may want to call a friend whose children attend the public school yours would attend if you chose to enroll them, and ask your friend for the district name. If all else fails, call the local public school near you and ask the receptionist for the name of the school district, but there is not need to give any additional information.

5. Street Address (P.O. Box is not acceptable) *and
6. City * [plus State and Zip]

You must enter your street address (physical location) even if you use a post office box for mail.

7. School Telephone Number *

You must enter your telephone number. There is a possibility that the CDE may need to call you as the administrator of your school, such as to verify information or make corrections. This is one reason to avoid having young children answer the phone, particularly during the first couple of months after filing.

CDS Code Numbers

The CDS code number is a unique identifying number assigned to private schools by the California Department of Education for statistical and tracking purposes. Private schools with five or fewer students have not been issued CDS code numbers since 1990. This is due entirely to budget restrictions on computer data entry. Not having a CDS code number does not affect the legal status of your private home-based school. If your private school does not have a CDS code number and it is requested (for instance, the CHSPE exam application form has a blank for your private school's CDS number) just write in "N/A" in the space provided.

Those who file affidavits with enrollments of six or more are assigned a CDS code number. If you have already received a CDS code number, it remains permanently for your school, even if your enrollment drops below six students. If you are filing a private school affidavit for the first time and your enrollment is six or more students, the California Department of Education will either send you a confirmation letter with your CDS code number, or they may call you to verify enrollment before issuing your school's CDS code number. Should you receive a call, simply verify the information you already submitted on your affidavit; do not reveal students' names or other information not on the affidavit form.

8. Optional Fax Number

Not required.

9. School Email Address (primary)*

10. Optional School Email Address

Not required.

11. Optional School Web Address

Not required.

12. Mailing Addess (required* if different from #5 above) and

13. Mailing City [plus State and Zip] (required* only if response in #12)

Having a separate mailing address is optional, but if you do have one, enter it here.

14. Type of School *

Mark "Coeducational" even if you currently have only boys or girls.

15. School Accommodations *

Mark "Day Only." Even though your children sleep at home, and your home is now a school, they sleep there because of its status as a home, not as a boarding school.

16. Does the school provide special education services?

Leave it checked as "no."

17. Range of Grades Offered *

A "Lowest" of 1 and a "Highest" of 12 is the best choice because it leaves you options for the future, although you can change your original designation in subsequent years. We do not recommend including kindergarten, since kindergarten is not mandatory in California and formally enrolling kindergarteners will generate additional paperwork from the Department of Health.

18. High School Diploma Offered *

Either answer, "Yes" or "No," is acceptable and you can change your answer in a later year. Do not indicate "Yes" unless you have indicated that you offer through grade 12. It is acceptable to say "Yes" even if your children are years away from graduation.

19. Classification of school

Most private home-based schools are not officially affiliated with nor under the authority of a denomination and therefore should check "Non-religious" or check "Religious" then select "not affiliated with any denomination" from the pull-down list.

Prior Year School Information

20. Has this school ever filed a Private School Affidavit under a different school name? *

This doesn't usually apply, so most will answer "No." But if you have changed your school name, and you filed last year under the old name, then mark "Yes."

21. Enter former name of school (if "Yes" answered to previous question)

Again, this doesn't usually apply, but if you changed your school name this year, enter the old name here.

22. Has this school changed public school districts? *

This doesn't usually apply, so most will answer "No." But if you have moved into a new school district since the time you filed your affidavit last year, check "Yes." This question most likely relates to the CDS code numbers that are assigned to schools with six or more students, since those numbers include a school district code.

23. Former public school district (if "Yes" answered to previous question)

Again, this doesn't usually apply, but if you moved to a new district since the time you filed last year's affidavit, enter the old school district here.

Statistical Information

24. Range of Students' Ages *

For the "youngest" field, type in the age of your youngest homeschooled child who is age six or older, and for the "oldest" field, type in the age of your oldest homeschooled child who is age 18 or younger. The range of your students' ages will obviously change each year.

25. Enrollment on a Single Date October 1-15, 2012 * (Note: Do not report pre-school enrollment; pre-schools that do not offer kindergarten should not file this PSA.)

The fields for enrollment numbers each have zero as a default. Simply change the number of pupils at each grade level to match the number of children you have enrolled in each grade level. If you do not "grade" your children, either select the grade levels that would match their ages if they were in a public school (i.e. six years old is typically first grade), or select "ungraded elementary" or "ungraded secondary."

The reason the instructions state to give the enrollment on a "single date" is that in large schools, enrollment can vary from day to day and this statistical information on your affidavit merely provides a snapshot of your school's enrollment at the time the affidavit is filed.

26. Number of Twelfth Grade Graduates in 2011-2012 School Year*

Note that this question asks about graduates for *last* year.

27. Number of School Staff *

Count each staff only once. In a two-parent private homeschool, you will probably have one administrator and one full-time teacher. It is common for administrators to also teach, so if the father is listed as site administrator in the "School Information" section, count him as an administrator here even though he also teaches the children.

<u>Administrative Staff</u>

28. Site Administrator *

For most homeschooling families, the parents are the administrators and directors of your school. Fill in the name of whichever one of you is taking the role of head administrator. Probably most common among homeschoolers is for the father's name to be listed here.

29. Site Administrator Title *

You can choose any of the titles, but most common among homeschoolers is for the father to be the site administrator and for his title to be "Principal."

30. Site Adminsitration Email Address*

This is required.

31. Director or Principal Officer Name *

This will most likely be the same person listed as "Site Administrator."

Preschoolers and Kindergartners

When listing grades offered or ages of enrolled children for your private school, do not indicate enrollment of any children who are under five years of age. The reason for this is that the California Department of Social Services, Community Care Licensing Division, rather than the Department of Education, has jurisdiction over the licensing of all private preschools and day-care centers for children younger than four years and nine months of age.

Also, while you will notice there is a space on the PSA form for the number of students enrolled in kindergarten, kindergarten is not mandatory in California. Therefore, if you have a child who is younger than compulsory school age (i.e., is not age six by September 1) do not enroll him in your school and do not count him on your affidavit. You may, of course, teach your children who are under compulsory attendance age at home. They simply are not formally enrolled in your private school.

32. Director or Principal Officer Position *

List the same title you listed for the Site Administrator, typically "Principal."

33. Director or Principal Officer Address * and

34. Director or Principal Officer City [plus State and Zip] *

For homeschoolers, this will be the same street address as your school address.

35. Director or Principal Officer Email Address

Not required.

School Records

36. Name of Individual Who Is Custodian of Records *

This is typically the same as the director or site administrator listed above.

37. Custodian of Records Address * and

38. Custodian of Records City [plus State and Zip] *

This is typically the same as the school address. Note that including the location of the school records does not imply that those records are open to inspection, unless the person requesting access has a court order or a warrant.

39. Custodian of Records E-mail Address

Not required.

Tax Status of School

40. through 43. Four boxes to choose from

For private homeschools, the appropriate choice is "None of the Above."

Acknowledgements and Statutory Notices *

Each box is required. Checking a box indicates your understanding of the statement and your school's compliance.

The form cannot be filed by computer unless all boxes for questions 44-54 are checked.

44. ☐ All Private School Affidavits are public documents viewable by the public.

This is just for your information. It's not common that someone would want to go view all the affidavits, but access to them is open.

45. ☐ The Private School Affidavit must be filed by persons, firms, associations, partnerships, or corporations offering or conducting full-time day school at the elementary or high school level for students between the ages of six and eighteen years of age.

This is just for your information. As a "person," you can file an affidavit.

46. ☐ Preschools should contact the Community Care Licensing Division (CCLD) of the California Department of Social Services. Contact CCLD at 916-229-4500 or contact a regional office.

This is just for your information. Operating a preschool is beyond the scope of these instructions. The Private School Affidavit is only for schools offering elementary or secondary instruction, which encompasses kindergarten and grades 1-12.

47. ☐ The Affidavit is not a license or authorization to operate a private school.

This is just for your information. You don't need a license and you don't need authorization to operate a private school.

48. ☐ The Private School Affidavit does not indicate approval, recognition, or endorsement by the state. Filing of this Affidavit shall not be interpreted to mean, and it shall be unlawful for any school to expressly or impliedly represent by any means whatsoever, that the State of California, the Superintendent of Public Instruction, the State Board of Education, the CDE, or any division or bureau of the Department, or any accrediting agency has made any evaluation, recognition, approval, or endorsement of the school or course unless this is an actual fact (see EC Section 33190).

This is just for your information. It's straight out of the Education Code and is simply meant to clarify that your filing of an affidavit does not mean you are approved by the State. However, you don't need State approval to operate a private school.

49. ☐ **Private school authorities are responsible for initiating contact with the appropriate local authorities (city and/or county) regarding compliance with ordinances governing health, safety and fire standards, business licensing, and zoning requirements applicable to private schools.**

This is just for your information. As a private homeschool, you're not running a business out of your home, so you won't need to contact any of these authorities.

50. ☐ **When a school ceases operation, every effort should be made to give a copy of pupils' permanent records to parents or guardians. If records cannot be given to the parents or guardians, it is recommended that the school's custodian of records retain the records permanently so that former pupils may obtain copies when needed for future education, employment, or other purposes.**

This is just for your information. If you ever stop homeschooling, be sure to check the instructions elsewhere in this manul for handling school records properly.

51. ☐ **Retain a copy of this document for a period of three years.**

This is just a recommendation, but it's a good one.

52. ☐ **Filing a Private School Affidavit is not equivalent to obtaining accreditation. A Private School Affidavit does not signify that any accrediting agency has made any evaluation, recognition, approval, or endorsement of the school or courses offered by the school.**

This is just for your information. Accreditation is not required of private schools.

53. ☐ **A private school shall not employ a person who has been convicted of a violent or serious felony or a person who would be prohibited from employment by a public school district pursuant to EC Section 44237. This school is in compliance with EC Section 44237 to the extent that it applies.**

This is just for your information since you probably do not have any employees for your private school. See the sidebar at right for more information on this topic.

54. ☐ **The students enrolled in this private school and included in the school's enrollment total are full-time students in this school and are not enrolled in any other public or private elementary or secondary school on a full-time basis.**

This is not actually required by the law. However, if your students don't attend a "full-time" private day school, your students are not exempt from compulsory attendance at public school. This doesn't mean they can't take some classes elsewhere, it just means that their enrollment status in your school is that of a full-time student. Most homeschoolers' children are enrolled as full-time students in their private homeschools, so this statement most likely applies to your students and you can check the box.

Background Checks

E.C. § 44237 requires criminal background checks. However, it "does not apply to a ... parent or legal guardian working exclusively with his or her children." It applies only to schools that employ someone for services rendered. However, this requirement also does not apply to those whom you may hire to teach music lessons, or the like, unless they are employees of your school.

Electronic Signature

By submitting this form and the electronic signature attached hereto, I declare under penalty of perjury and the laws of the State of California that I am the owner or other head of the school, and the information contained herein is true, accurate, and complete.

Name of owner or other head of school *

This should be the same person that you listed in Questions 28 and 30.

Title *

Use the same title you used previously for the Director or Principal Officer in Question 31.

Telephone Number *

Electronic Signature - Birth Month *

Electronic Signature - Birthday *

Electronic Signature - Question *

Electronic Signature - Answer *

This information is required to verify the electronic "signature." Choose one of the security questions, which will allow you to access your school's information in the future.

Submit Form

Click on the "Submit Form" button at the bottom of the online affidavit. Your completed form with a confirmation number at the bottom will be displayed.

Print a copy of the completed affidavit form for your file. Keep the copy in your school file for three years. Affidavits that are completed and submitted to the CDE online do not need to be physically signed and copies should not be mailed to the CDE after your affidavit has been submitted electronically.

What If Your School Information Changes After You File the PSA?

If information from your affidavit changes during the year, you do not need to notify the CDE or change your affidavit form. The changes will simply be made on next year's affidavit. If you discontinue homeschooling during the school year, you also do not need to notify the CDE. Not filing an affidavit next year will indicate to the CDE that your school is no longer operating.

Chapter Three

Choices in Schooling

Teaching Methods

Your philosophy of home education will affect how you teach and what curriculum you use. If you skipped the Philosophy of Education section, you are urged to go back and read it now.

Whoever introduced you to the subject of home education probably also introduced you to their own approach to teaching and learning. You may have even assumed that there is only one way to teach and that all textbooks are geared toward this approach. Rather than just assume your friend's approach is the right one for you, it is more beneficial to your homeschool to learn something about the various approaches. Then you can decide, based on your educational philosophy and your children's learning styles, which one or ones would be best for you and your family.

Eleven major approaches to education are presented in this chapter. In reality there are many more, to say nothing of a tremendous variety of ways to mix these, but introducing these will demonstrate the myriad ways to homeschool. As you gain experience and confidence, and as your philosophy becomes more clear, your approach will likely change.

A list of resources is found in the appendix. Some of the listed companies sell a wide variety of materials, suitable for many different teaching methods and learning styles. Others cater to one method. Thus, you will need to look carefully at their catalogs and determine whether their materials will fit your homeschool.

Traditional/Conventional Textbooks

You are probably most familiar with the traditional or conventional textbook approach. These are the same as or similar to texts and materials used in campus-based Christian schools.

Each publishing company has a unique point of view or focus that you will want to investigate for compatibility with your educational philosophy, but most Christian textbook publishers are dedicated to a Christian bias.

These texts are available directly from the publisher or sometimes through distributors. The books come in hard or soft covers; curriculum guides, teacher's manuals, textbooks, and answer keys are available.

This method usually requires active parent involvement for maximum understanding—you will need to write lesson plans, discuss the material with your student, assign reports or projects, administer tests, and evaluate progress. However, some parents may find themselves merely issuing reading assignments, leaving the child in a self-teaching mode. Progressing through the material is usually along traditional lines: first grade material in first grade, etc. However, you as the teacher decide how fast or slow the student goes.

Delayed Formal Academics

Another well-known approach is delayed formal academics. Proponents delay formal academics until the student reaches his integrated maturity level (IML), which is anywhere from age seven to eleven. Before this time the emphasis is on practical experience, hands-on projects, and parents reading aloud non-fiction books to children. There is an emphasis on household participation, family business, and service projects.

When the student's vision, hearing, nervous system, reasoning ability, and muscular co-ordination have sufficiently developed (i.e., they have reached their IML), short periods of supervised study are added, usually along the lines of unit or integrated studies.

The idea is to not push before the child is ready, but to take advantage of the child's development. The child is exposed to a variety of activities and learns quickly when he is ready. The emphasis is on readiness, informal learning, and warm, responsive parental involvement.

Early Childhood Academics

Seemingly opposite of delayed formal academics is the early childhood academics approach. Proponents believe that since structure and obedience to God's laws are an integral part of the Christian life, they should be taught early with formal academic training. They believe a child's character is formed during the first six years and spiritual, moral, and academic development is critical during this time. They believe this structure trains children to be receivers of what they should learn rather than allowing them to develop the habit of doing only what they want.

Structured teaching times are geared to each child's attention span and abilities. However, proponents believe children by age four should regularly be doing some workbook exercises and by age five be doing a complete course of study.

This approach teaches every subject from its foundation in Scripture with Christ the center of the entire curriculum.

The early childhood academics and the delayed formal academics approaches each stress teaching what is appropriate to the child's attention span, ability, and maturation timetable. The two approaches, however, do seem to disagree on when that level is achieved in most children.

Ruth Beechick's Approach

Dr. Ruth Beechick , an educator and author, seems to have found a balance between the previous two methods. She gives parents common sense ways to teach their young children using age-appropriate methods without a lot of textbooks.

She has written a set of books on teaching the Three Rs (*A Fast Start in Reading*, *A Strong Start in Language*, and *An Easy Start in Arithmetic*, now available in one combined book) which give parents tools to teach early elementary children the important academic foundation with informal methods. Upper elementary grade children can also be taught with natural methods and less textbooks. In *You Can Teach Your Child Successfully* (Grades 4 - 8), Dr. Beechick recommends in language, for example, having children copy paragraphs from great literature, first using a hard copy and then writing from dictation. After writing the excerpt, there is discussion on the grammar, punctuation, vocabulary, etc. For history, she recommends reading good biographies and historical fiction in place of a lot of boring textbooks.

Worktexts/Mastery Learning

Worktexts are consumable workbooks that include both the text for the subject and frequent questions (with space provided for the answers), projects, or other assignments. Some companies that publish worktexts are better than others at including questions that take thought and application of concepts. There are tests or checkpoints to help the teacher know whether the student has learned (mastered) the material. When the material has been mastered, the student moves on.

Since lessons are already prepared, there is minimal preparation for the parent.

Some worktext curriculums have students set their own goals and some have parents set the goals based on the child's ability. Some subjects are condensed and not very detailed, but that could be an advantage depending on the goals of the parent and student.

Also, these mostly black and white worktexts with a distinct lack of photographs have a tendency to be visually boring. But again, this could be an advantage for those who cannot handle distractions.

Mastery learning advocate J. Richard Fugate, former president of Alpha Omega Publications says,

> Proper use of mastery learning requires the careful placement of the student where he is able to learn, reasonable but strictly enforced daily goals, continuous monitoring of work in progress by the teacher, and proficiency testing to determine results. ... The process of mastery learning ensures success for each student, thus developing a positive attitude toward education as well as self-confidence. ... The fact that mastery learning is utilized by some educators

with evil intent to program humanistic socio-political conditioning in the public classroom does not mean that the concept of mastery learning is intrinsically evil.with evil intent to program humanistic socio-political conditioning in the public classroom does not mean that the concept of mastery learning is intrinsically evil.

Charlotte Mason's Approach

Charlotte Mason was a teacher, author, and lecturer in England in the late 19th and early 20th Century. Charlotte Mason has said of her views:

> The children are respected and accepted as valid persons. But they are not left on the island of their own limited resources. Through careful choice, they are nourished with the best we human beings have to offer: mind is introduced to mind, child to nature and activities. Pray that our children may be so educated in a total life that they are enabled to have clear, realistic, and true thinking and action based on thought and principle. May they be strong personalities, free of self and external pressures so that they will have the power to do what is right.

The essence of her approach is that children should develop a "noble character" and "a fine mind," rather than "playing at education." This approach includes creating an atmosphere of freedom for exploration and individuality, but balanced with an emphasis on developing habits and routines, such as concentration, truthfulness, self-control, and unselfishness.

Mason's approach includes spending the morning working on chores, math and reading skills, followed by reading and discussing real books with "living ideas." There is much emphasis on spending afternoons in nature with time for play and creative endeavors. After reading the "living books," the child narrates the story back to the parent and discusses the ideas presented. These methods were designed to help children see and understand the principles and ideas behind the knowledge gained.

Unit Study Approach

Also known as integrated studies, the unit study approach blends all subjects around a common theme or project. This approach is based on a belief that all knowledge is inter-related, is learned more readily, and is retained longer when presented as a "whole."

The amount and type of themes are endless, but include such things as individual character qualities, plants, animals, earth, exploration, Indians, etc. Each unit study may take a few weeks to a couple of months and for each unit includes reading books (fiction, non-fiction, biographies), writing reports, hands-on projects, art, etc. Usually the history and the scientific background or explanations are included.

All ages can study a topic together with a variety of projects for the appropriate age level. There are many programs available that provide topic suggestions along with project instructions, reading lists, etc. This approach usually needs to be supplemented with math instruction.

Delight Directed Study

Another approach using unit study projects is Gregg Harris' approach called delight directed study. The concept is based on the parent demonstrating his wisdom and delight in learning by involving his children in his activities, assigning study projects for developing skills and knowledge. As this pattern is furthered, the children will develop their own delights and interests, which are the basis for further projects and studies.

An eight-week period is usually divided into 10 to 12 projects, including all areas of academic study. For example, if the subject is baseball, projects and subjects covered could include: write a brief history of baseball (research, composition, spelling, history); interview a local sportscaster (planning questions, arranging interview, speech, note taking); read a biography of a Major League player and write a report (reading, writing, history); compare salaries of early and modern players (research, math, history); make a glossary of terms and learn to spell (vocabulary, spelling); the biblical perspective of the sport or skills involved; to name just a few possible projects on one subject.

The Principle Approach

The principle approach is based on three unique themes: the recognition of God's Hand or Providence in history; the biblical principles of civil and self-government; and thinking governmentally (emphasizing personal responsibility for extending the government of God into all areas of life). The method of teaching these themes is called the 4Rs: Researching (biblical principles and purposes); Reasoning from these truths; Relating the principles to the student's character, talents, etc.; and Recording in writing the applications to the individual.

Proponents describe this method as "America's historic Christian method of biblical reasoning, which makes the Truths of God's Word the basis of every subject in the school curriculum."

This method enables the Christian teacher who can reason from a biblical philosophy to take possession of the principles, ideas, and facts of a subject, using a variety of textbooks, references, and original resources.

Curriculum guides and resources are available.

Classical Approach

This approach originated in Ancient Greece and has survived to modern times. It focuses on teaching the tools of learning to study any subject. These tools are known as the Trivium (grammar stage, dialectic [logic] stage, and rhetoric [creative use of language] stage) followed by the study of the Quadrivium (arithmetic, geometry, astronomy, and music).

This approach was modernized by the English writer Dorothy Sayers, who modified it into a system that teaches these subjects concurrently but divided into phases that correspond to the three stages of the Trivium begun at strategic points in the mental development of the child.

Mrs. Sayers wrote,

> although we often succeed in teaching our pupils 'subjects,' we fail lamentably on the whole in teaching them how to think: they learn everything, except the art of learning. ... For the sole true end of education is simply this: to teach men how to learn

for themselves; and whatever instruction fails to do this is effort spent in vain.

Unschooling Approach

The most famous advocate of this approach is the late John Holt, author of many books on education, including *Teach Your Own*, in which he wrote: "What children need is not new and better curricula but access to more and more of the real world; plenty of time and space to think over their experiences, and to use fantasy and play to make meaning out of them; and advice, road maps, guidebooks, to make it easier for them to get where they want to go (not where we think they ought to go), and to find out what they want to find out." His conclusion is that children's natural curiosity and desire to learn is destroyed by today's teaching methods.

Definitely child-centered, this approach assumes that children can be trusted to direct their own learning and they know what they need from their parent. The parent's responsibility is to: (1) model a life of interest and exploration; (2) involve their children in adult activities; (3) surround the children with a rich environment of books and resources for learning; and (4) respond to children's questions, interests, and concerns.

This approach assumes that children will learn whatever they need to know when the need arises. However, Scripture teaches, "a child left to himself brings his mother shame." Moreover, neither parents nor children have the wisdom to direct their own paths. We need God's guidance and children need their parent's guidance and training.

The advantage of this approach is that when working with the child's interests and talents, information is learned and retained better. However, self-centeredness may be the result.

Conclusion

Most home educators use a personalized blend of these approaches to properly meet the needs of their family. As a home educator you have the privilege and responsibility to investigate and follow the most appropriate means of education for your children.

Learning Styles

Entire books are written and semester-long courses are taught on learning styles. Just as each person has a distinct personality, each person has a preferred, or natural, way of learning. There are four basic learning styles or methods. Some educators have broken these four down to many sub-types. You will see how the different teaching methods might apply to the different learning styles. This discussion will be limited to the four basic styles.

As you read this section, you will recognize your own learning style. Be cautious that you don't impose your style on your children. As you consider the different learning styles, you will also see that few children fit solely in one category. Although there is a predominant learning style, another style may also be evident. You will also have a combination of learning styles in your family. What will work for one child, may not work for another. Sometimes it is a balancing act to accommodate the differences within the family.

Spontaneous

Action, action, action describes this learner. These are children who work for a short while then are up to the bathroom, refrigerator, or window. They like physical involvement, performances, and competitions. A fast-paced discussion is preferred over lectures and reading. Paper-and-pencil tasks are deadly to the spontaneous learner. Not only do they not plan well, they also want to know the value of the material NOW. Curriculum that has action, and even some risk, is best suited for these learners. They will tolerate quiet work for a time, when an activity is promised after the specified work time.

Routine

In a word, these learners thrive on structure. Routine learners need to know what is expected of them and tend not to be spontaneous. They will sit, listen, and take notes. This is the workbook learner, who enjoys just the act of completing and finds it a challenge. They will search diligently for facts and enjoy doing arithmetic problems, memorizing spelling words, and learning facts in history and science. These children are not bored with repetition. Not surprisingly, routine learners tend to be business majors or CPAs.

Conceptual

Conceptual learners are not interested in focusing on facts, but would rather interpret the facts. These children will usually follow-up a lecture or assignment by seeking answers to their own questions. Although they like long-term assignments, they prefer oral presentations to written and really enjoy sharing what they learn. Conceptual learners like small group discussions and tend to be debaters.

Global

This is the creative and independent learner. When given an assignment, these children will find their own material and their own way to complete it. They are not good with details and need repetition for detailed learning such as math facts. Although global learners enjoy small group discussions, they prefer written assignments. They also find workbooks to be deadly.

Choosing Curriculum

As you can imagine, there are as many different types of curriculum as there are teaching methods and learning styles. Following are the more popular curriculum types. A list of different companies is in the "Resources" section in the appendix..

Once you select curriculum each year, it's a good idea to create a master list of all the materials you plan to use. Many parents combine the curriculum list with their course of study, resulting in one document that shows what will be taught during the year and what materials will be used.

Traditional Textbooks

These are the textbooks most of us who attended a traditional classroom school remember. Most of these materials are designed for classroom teaching and may include a lot of "busy" work and other things you don't need in a homeschool.

Some companies sell traditional textbooks in complete packages for each grade level. These are very complete, right down to pencils in some cases. Daily lesson plans are often included and are set up for a 180-day school year.

Because the books are available in hardback editions, they are durable and last from year to year.

Worktexts

Although designed for independent learning, the more popular worktext curriculums were originally developed for classrooms. They are often used in small Christian schools.

The materials are consumable and relatively inexpensive. Most worktext programs have a series of booklets per subject for each grade level. This curriculum type requires little teacher preparation and the teacher's guides are written for those who may be unfamiliar with the subject.

It is possible to order one or two worktexts, instead of an entire year's worth, to see if this method works for you and your children. Because the worktexts are consumable, it can be tempting to photocopy the booklets for each student, but that is a violation of copyright laws.

Unit Study

Unit studies are very flexible and can accommodate different age groups and a variety of learning styles. Although the up-front cost may be high, unit study materials can be used for several years.

A lot of preparation is required by the parent. Often supplemental materials are needed for math and language arts. Most companies that provide unit studies offer sample lessons.

Computer Aided

These are software programs that help with teaching. Some are very good, and others are merely games described as "edutainment."

Some traditional textbook and worktext companies have now developed their materials in the form of computer software. Generally these are the paper versions on CD-ROMS with automatic scoring.

Online

Online education is one of the fastest growing approaches. Some websites offer free classes, while others offer complete online programs that can be expensive.

Some of these programs still require textbooks. The quality varies from very good programs to some which are a waste of time. Check out the program thoroughly, including working through sample lessons.

There are several charter schools that offer online programs. Before enrolling, be sure to find out whether it is a public school program online.

Living Books

Living books refers to classic literature, well-written biographies, and other books that make a subject come to life for the student.

Laura Ingalls Wilder's *Little House on the Prairie* series is a good example. Students learn about a time period of history through reading a book that makes them feel like they are there, as opposed to reading a dry textbook.

These materials are available from many publishers, and also can be found for free at your local public or church library.

Real Tools

Many homeschoolers enjoy being able to use "real tools" and practical experiences to teach various subjects, as opposed to using curriculum which includes assignments to be completed by the student at his desk.

The public school counterpart is lab courses such as cooking, chemistry, or wood working. Homeschoolers can consider a wider variety of real tools for use in more of their courses, since they don't have the expense of supplying such things to a classroom of thirty or more children.

For example, a good sewing machine or set of woodworking tools may be included in the curriculum budget. Besides the obvious subject areas, students can learn math, business skills, character development, reading, and more through the use of such equipment.

Chapter Four

You're the Teacher, Now What?

Scheduling

For some parents, the idea of yearly scheduling and planning seems daunting, not to mention what appears to be a mountain of paperwork for recordkeeping. By using a systematic approach, no matter the teaching method you choose, the task will be easier.

Before you can start planning lessons or keeping records, you need to consider a schedule. You need to take into consideration the ages of your children and your other family activities. It should be noted that the younger the child, the less formal the schedule should be. In fact, rather than thinking of it as a "schedule" for preschool or elementary children, think of a routine. Otherwise, your the child may be no better off at home than in a formal classroom. The young child has a greater need to learn from natural, everyday activities, rather than doing formal book work.

As for older children, philosophies vary greatly as to how structured scheduling should be. Some homes have a very structured program quite similar to a regular school day. Other homes are able to accomplish the same goals and cover the same territory with a very flexible approach. The type of teaching method may also determine how structured your schedule will be. It may take until the second year to really hit your stride. Homeschooling requires flexibility, structure, and a creative touch. Some parents tend to be overly structured the first year or two to be better able to defend their choice of home educating.

You must decide what is best for you, probably by trial and error. When there are multiple grades, scheduling calls for some real creativity. But that creative touch and the flexibility it requires is one of the things that makes homeschool fun. You can expect that it will take a year or two to feel comfortable with your schedule.

Schedule Ideas

Some homeschools concentrate on basics four days a week and spend the fifth on art, music, field trips, home living skills or other non-academic studies. Many go to the library weekly.

You may teach each subject every day or on alternate days. Some find a college-type schedule more successful — some subjects are taught Monday-Wednesday-Friday and others Tuesday-Thursday. Other homeschoolers teach one subject each day (e.g., math on Monday, language on Tuesday, history on Wednesday, etc.) These methods give you more time each day to go into subjects in more depth and to use the aids you will no doubt acquire. The variations are really endless as long as you reach your goals.

Some older children make great tutors for their younger siblings, helping in a variety of ways, such as giving spelling tests, grading papers, testing with flash cards, etc.

Parents show much creativity in designing special small group classes such as values, character qualities, or vocabulary development. Where you have a gift, use it. Where you see a need, fill it. Contrary to what some may think, home education need not be done in isolation. Draw on local resources such as your homeschool group, library, or museums.

Since there is no required number of days for each school year, you can set your own yearly schedule. Some families follow a traditional nine-month schedule while others plan a year-round schedule. Many parents are experiencing success with year-round school which features shorter, but more frequent vacations. One creative schedule includes school three weeks each month with a week off. Or, six weeks on, followed by one or two off. Families are also able to make a schedule that works for their family around father's work schedule. Others find it easier to follow the public school calendar, if that is what their children are already used to.

Lesson Plans

Lesson planning begins with deciding where each child is academically and spiritually. You can then decide where to go (goals) and how to get there (methods).

It is best to begin with a general idea of your school year; that is, what days or weeks you will teach and what days or weeks you plan to take off for vacation. Plan this on a Proposed School Year Calendar, use it while lesson planning, and then file it with your teaching records.

Start with a yearly plan: what subjects are you going to teach, and if some will some be half-year, while others are full-year. Decide what will be taught in the fall or in the spring. Remember, during the holidays you'll want to plan less schoolwork to allow time for the extra holiday activities. After you have set your yearly plan, you can divide it into four quarters or into other smaller units. How much do you think you can cover in each quarter?

At the beginning of each quarter or other session, divide the subjects by weeks. Your overall yearly schedule will determine how many weeks you will be planning for. You will now have a time line for each week. Then, at the beginning of your week, you can divide the work by the days—however you plan your days.

The most common way to plan traditional textbook lessons (but not necessarily the only or best way) is to select a textbook at the appropriate level, determine how much of the textbook (which chapters or topics) you want to cover, and plan how many weeks (days, months) it will take. For example, you may want to cover all but the last two chapters of a 38-chapter history book. You then begin with 36 chapters to be covered over a traditional 36-week school year. That leaves you with one chapter a week to be covered. If you have a history lesson four days a week, you divide each chapter into fourths. Your lesson plan will then reflect those pages that equal approximately one-fourth of a chapter. You can plan this out at the beginning of the year, adding in the details such as projects, reports, field trips, etc.

This plan never seems to work out as smoothly as it sounds, unless you build in some extra time for emergencies, new ideas, etc. For example, you may be better off deciding to cover 36 chapters in 30 weeks for a 36-week school year. This will give you six weeks leeway for adding in extra special opportunities and surprises that arise, family vacations, illnesses, etc.

If you are not using traditional textbooks, you still need to decide how many weeks for school, how many weeks you want to plan for, and what projects you want to do for each subject and how much time each will take.

You can fill in the finer details as you go along. From these subject lesson plans you can extract a weekly lesson plan, and perhaps from that an assignment sheet for each student.

Grading

One of the most intimidating jobs is fairly and accurately evaluating a student's progress. Questions of competence and objectivity can make you feel unable or unqualified to determine progress and assign a grade. With proper understanding and practice, however, any parent can learn to issue grades that are fair and truly reflect the student's progress.

The main ingredient in evaluating progress is constant observation. In order to issue a grade on progress made, you need to know where the student began, what his strengths and weaknesses are, how well the information is being assimilated, and whether the original goal has been attained. A parent can know this by observation throughout the learning process. You have a real advantage in this area over classroom teachers. Rather than getting to know new students each year and trying to assess their strengths, weaknesses, study habits, and ability to learn, you already know your students and will be observing them over an extended period of time.

The most difficult part of grading is setting realistic goals. Trying to achieve too much will produce frustration and unrealistically low grades. Setting goals that are too low will result in student boredom and grades that may be high but reflect little real learning. When you know your child's strengths and weaknesses, setting goals becomes easier. Expecting more from a child in areas of strength will help develop God-given talents. These goals would then be higher than in areas of weakness. Goals in weak areas would reflect the degree of help needed to strengthen those weak areas.

Once goals are set in each subject, there are three areas that can assist you in arriving at a final grade. These are: 1) attendance, 2) participation and work completion, and 3) test grades and knowledge retention. Once again, you have an advantage over the typical classroom teacher, since you don't have to rely exclusively on testing and homework completion.

Attendance is absolutely necessary to get the most understanding out of a lesson. In the home setting, your student may be absent some days; however, this does not mean missing material. The lesson is postponed until the next session. Each student gets full credit for attendance at all lessons.

Participation is also necessary to master material, and this is easy to monitor in a home setting. Has your student read all of the material and listened to your explanations? Was each assignment completed on time? Was the work up to the student's ability, including penmanship and grammar? It is important to remember each child's ability will be different and progress should not be evaluated against others. Progress will be different for a gifted student than for a slow student, or for a student with good small-muscle coordination than for a student with poor coordination. An understanding of stages of development in a child is helpful here.

An important consideration is attitude, that is, heart attitude. Was your student cheerful and cooperative? Is the work seen as a call from God? Or, on the other hand, is there rebellion against the work, laziness, or trying to get out of the work? The character qualities developed and habits begun during learning sessions will remain for a lifetime and are key to what you are trying to teach.

Testing and knowledge retention is the last ingredient which will help you confidently judge progress. Testing can mean oral or written examination, or it can be completion of a project or a presentation. The goal is to assess comprehension and retention of the material presented. The methods used to determine retention should vary with age, maturity, and personality. Once again you have the best opportunity to make an accurate judgment of your student's progress. Testing need not be limited to the written or timed variety. Using different methods can produce a more accurate reflection of how well the material has been mastered.

There are several systems for assigning grades to a student. The most widely used, and recommended for high school students who are planning to apply to college or university, is the letter grades A, B, C, D, F. A letter grade can be arrived at by considering the words which they represent: A=Outstanding, B=Very Good, C=Average, D=Needs Improvement but passing, and F=Failure or needs to repeat the material. Grades can also be awarded by grading each assignment or test on a percentage basis: A=90-100%, B=80-89%, C=70-79%, D=60-69%, and F=below 60%. An alternate to giving D's or F's, is the use of R for "repeat the material."

There are clever little grading slides which figure all of these percentages for a teacher. Several varieties are usually available from local teacher supply stores and homeschool curriculum suppliers. Online grading tools are also available on the Internet.

Other "non-letter grade" grading models are Pass/Fail, Complete/Incomplete, or O=Outstanding/E=Excellent, S=Satisfactory, U=Unsatisfactory or N=Needs Improvement These are traditionally reserved for younger elementary grades.

You should award grades at least once each year for elementary students (the non-letter grades are fine) and once each semester or year for junior and senior high students (preferably using a letter grading system). High school students should also be awarded credits for each course they complete; see CHEA's *High School Handbook*, by Mary Schofield, for guidelines.

The grades awarded each year or semester are what you include in the student's cum file. These become part of the student's permanent record which stays with him if he transfers to another school. For high school students, the semester or yearly grades go on a transcript which is sent to colleges when it's time to apply.

A final comment about grading: the world puts too much emphasis on comparing students' progress with one another (the norms in standardized testing, for example). As Christian home educators, we best serve our Lord and our children by judging their work individually. "And behold, I come quickly; and my reward is with me, to give every man according as his work shall be" (Rev. 22:12).

Unless you adhere to a very structured schedule and allow your child to advance only one grade level a year, you will soon find that your child is working on several grade levels at once. After a few years you may even forget about grade levels and think instead in terms of mastery and progression of materials. However, for the convenience of being able to answer questions or fill out various forms asking for grade level, families usually refer to the appropriate grade for their child's age.

If you wish to promote your child at the end of each year, or as is commonly done, after sixth or eighth grade, there are many creative ways to honor your child. Some support groups have a recognition ceremony to which friends and families are invited. Blank awards and certificates can be purchased from school supply stores or curriculum publishers, or created on your computer.

Achievement Tests

Achievement testing, especially for younger children, is an area of controversy. Some parents feel it necessary to give their children standardized tests, while others believe it is unnecessary or even potentially destructive.

In deciding whether to have your children take achievement tests, you should consider what you hope to accomplish. Taking a test just because others are doing so is not a great reason. You also should understand that there is no law in California requiring any kind of tests for private school children. Thus the decision of whether to have your children take tests at all is entirely up to you.

Those who favor achievement testing say it is a good way to measure academic progress. As a homeschooler, you're certainly able to tell whether your child can read or spell or complete his math lesson accurately, but you may find it harder to pinpoint specific problems. Many homeschoolers are also concerned about undiscovered gaps in their children's education and believe achievement tests can show weak areas that could then become a focus of future study. Finally, testing can be one way to demonstrate the success of your school to anyone who might question you.

Those who choose not to use achievement tests state they do not provide dependable or helpful results because many bright children do not test well. Additionally, auditory or kinesthetic learners are at a disadvantage when taking written exams. Another disadvantage may be that standardized tests are geared toward children in a classroom setting with a specific curriculum. Also, test results may be invalidated because the child has simply had a bad day. Finally, the time spent studying for and taking standardized exams is not worth the minimal benefit.

Diagnostic Tests

In addition to achievement testing, diagnostic testing is also available. This type of testing is particularly useful when learning problems are suspected. Diagnostic testing does not focus on academic skills or progress through various grade levels of material. Instead, it focuses on learning skills and abilities such as visual and auditory learning, reasoning, attention span, etc., with an aim of detecting learning disabilities or similar challenges. Whether or not you favor achievement tests, if you suspect that your child may have a learning disability, a good diagnostic test by a skilled professional may provide valuable assistance as you continue to teach your child.

Availability of Standardized Tests

Due to concern for the validity of test results, most testing companies have tightened control on who may obtain and administer standardized tests. This makes testing sources scarcer and makes it unlikely that you'll be able to administer one of these tests to your own children.

Achievement or diagnostic tests are available through some PSPs. Some PSPs will allow you to take an exam through them even if your children are not enrolled, though there will likely be a fee. Even some private Christian campus-based schools educators may help with testing. Many private psychologists or educators also do testing. Ask your local homeschool leader who is recommended in your area, or call a couple of local private Christian schools to ask.

There are other tests, such as the California High School Proficiency Exam (CHSPE), college admissions exams, advanced placement exams, and more, which are commonly taken by high school students. More specific help in all areas of teaching high school students at home can be found in the *High School Handbook*, available from CHEA.

Portfolios

A portfolio is simply samples of work. Artists, writers, designers, and musicians often have portfolios to be able to present their work to prospective clients or employers. A portfolio of your student's work, especially high school work, may be a better indicator of acquired knowledge and skills than grades or test scores, especially for the student who doesn't test well. Some colleges may ask for a portfolio of a home-educated student's work in addition to other application documents.

A portfolio is not hard to create. One method is to add one item each month during the school year. The overall collection of work should be representative of all the subjects taken that year and should demonstrate educational growth. At the end of the year, these papers can be stored in a binder.

Along with obvious items like great essays, which can be included as-is, you may want to use photographs or journals to record labs, big projects, and field trips. Special honors, awards, and recognition of service can also be included in an academic portfolio.

At the end of high school, the portfolio can be bound in a permanent book and presented to the student upon graduation. Office supply stores often provide binding services, or look online for resources. Good quality photo albums, scrapbooks, or nice notebook binders are good substitutes. Also, check at your local art supply store for ideas.

If your child has a special interest such as art or sports, a separate portfolio for that interest should be made. This can include samples of work, certificates of achievement and awards, and letters of recommendation. In the case of sports, a list of teams, coaches, positions played, and honors achieved should be included.

Portfolios can be used for scholarship applications, especially if the scholarship is related to an area of special interest. Always check with the college or scholarship organization before submitting your portfolio.

Chapter Five

Special Seasons,
Special Children

Preschoolers

Considering God's different plan for each child, it should be no surprise that, despite many similarities, each child develops and learns differently.

In the years between two and six there is often a two-year variance in abilities and readiness to learn certain tasks. This is normal. A child may be quite advanced in one area and yet not in several other areas. Use these years as a time to teach a love for the Lord and important character traits such as obedience, helpfulness, and self control, knowing the child will more easily learn other skills which require a certain degree of readiness when that readiness has been reached. Preschool is the time to build a foundation of faith, values, morals, and manners.

Your child will grow and learn if you are personally involved, take advantage of teachable moments, and incorporate an atmosphere of discovery into your home and daily activities. This is true teaching as suggested by Deuteronomy 6:5-7.

> You shall love the Lord your God with all your heart, with all your soul, and with all your strength.
>
> And these words which I command you today shall be in your heart.
>
> You shall teach them diligently to your children, and shall talk of them when you sit in your house, when you walk by the way, when you lie down, and when you rise up (Deuteronomy 6:5-7 NKJV).

Making Your Foundation Strong

There is nothing more important in the preschool years than building a strong sense of being a family in Christ. Little children require vast amounts of time, and parents find themselves needing to let go of other interests for a season in order to devote time to the children. While you are in the midst of dealing with demanding little ones, it can feel as if it will never end. But it is amazing how quickly this time will pass. Use these years to build the kind of family you desire.

Loving God

One of the best things about having your children home with you is the gift of time. There is no need to herd everyone out the door each morning and no rush to fit the day's needs and activities into the evening. This freedom allows plenty of time for sharing God's Word with your children, which in today's busy world is a rare and priceless opportunity. Some parents read the Bible, even the King James Version, to their preschoolers. Children hearing the King James Version often develop beautiful vocabularies and manners of speech because they have heard them daily. Other parents read Bible storybooks. You can do both.

For memory work, a variety of simple materials is available. Scripture Memory Fellowship has lovely illustrated scripture memory books for preschoolers. Some children can repeat and remember anything they hear, so be in tune with your child's abilities and teach what you can.

Your Philosophy

Beginning your homeschool efforts in the preschool years gives you the opportunity to build a Christian worldview and develop a philosophy of education. You can take this time to learn to think in a way that is consistent with Scripture before you advance to teaching more rigorous academics. This is particularly true for those raised in non-Christian homes and public school backgrounds.

Your worldview is the way you understand God, man, and man's relationship to God. It must be based on the truth of Scripture. God's Word and your worldview affect the choices you make in your daily life. For example, if your child, (as many five-year-olds do) develops a fascination for dinosaurs, you will need biblically based answers to questions about where dinosaurs fit into the framework of God's creation. You may need to research to find specific answers that fit with Scripture, and you may need to relearn some things you were taught while you were in school.

Some questions you may want to take time to consider during the preschool years include, "How do children learn best?" "What makes the best atmosphere for children to grow and thrive?" "What about the issue of TV?" "What place do our Christian beliefs have in education?" and "Do children learn best through real life experiences?"

Learning Through Daily Life

Daily life offers many opportunities for teaching your child. You have already done this from the time he was born, teaching him to hold still while you change his diapers, to dress himself, to put his toys in the basket, not to touch the hot stove, and more. Involving your child in your daily routine gives your child a sense of belonging and pride in his family and home.

Schedules

Children are more comfortable with routine in the home. An easy way to begin is to have Bible time after breakfast and before bedtime. Add a rest time after lunch and you have a routine.

Other families prefer to have Bible time after breakfast. You and your children may find that another sequence works better for you, and you may want more or less of a routine. Because each family is different due to the parents' work hours, the children's sleeping habits, and other demands, there is no one way to devise a schedule. However, it helps if you stay home as often as possible and have some sort of regularity to your day.

Teaching routine household chores is an excellent way to teach obedience. Chores have immediate rewards: when you wash the dishes, they are clean. A child learns the benefits of doing what needs to be done and the value of effort. As he grows older and begins formal lessons, he will already understand his effort will produce results. By the time a child is six, he can do most household chores, although not as well as an adult. Having children for house-keepers means your home may not be as clean as you would like, and teaching and training takes more time than doing it yourself. However, having children who know how to work hard, work as a team, and contribute something valuable and real to the household is worth the patience. Thirty minutes a day spent cleaning together will help you stay on top of the work.

Learning Academic Skills

Academic skills are addressed last because they are the least important skills your child learns as a preschooler. A few children will make it clear that they are ready to learn some academic skills, but it can be done in a casual informal way. If your child says he wants to make a picture for Grandma and then asks how to write "I love you," you can show him how to write "I love you." You do not need formal lessons at this age.

This section was adapted from *Preschool at Home — What do I do with my child before kindergarten?*, by Debbie Feely, available from CHEA.

High School

Teaching high school students at home is not as difficult as some may fear. It does bring its own special difficulties; however, the rewards can be said to be proportionate with those obstacles. Additionally, teaching high school students at home brings with it a larger and somewhat different set of recordkeeping challenges. The good news is that there is help.

The High School Handbook, available from CHEA, covers setting up a solid high school program, including planning, areas of study, graduation requirements and methods, high school credits, choosing and designing high school courses, course descriptions and standards, resources, college and other post high school opportunities, transcripts, and much more.

Can You Teach High School Subjects?

Homeschooling parents are sometimes concerned that they are not qualified to teach certain subjects. For this reason, some enroll their high school students in a traditional school. However, since thousands of students graduate each year from private homeschools and go on to college, military, or the business world with few difficulties, you should proceed with confidence. In all likelihood, your children will succeed as well.

You can opt to teach all subjects at home or make use of outside resources, like group classes with other homeschoolers, private tutors, a local private high school, or a community college for courses you do not want to teach yourself. You may find that another homeschool parent in your area can speak and teach a foreign language, or that a local engineer would be willing to tutor your student in advanced math. And don't overlook any Christian colleges in your area. They will often allow sharp high school students to take a class or two, especially during summer.

Parents also tackle the "hard" classes, such as lab sciences or foreign language after receiving their own training at a convention. The CHEA Conventions offer this type of teacher training to thousands of parents each year.

High School Graduation

Some parents worry that their child needs to graduate from an accredited high school. Accreditation is a process by which schools guarantee they meet specific standards of the accrediting agency. There is no one agency that gives this approval and some public high schools are not accredited. While some colleges and employers may require an accredited diploma, it's not a common requirement.

Remember that "graduation" means completion of a high school course of study. If you run a private school, you will have the job of determining what the required course of study is for your student to complete for graduation.

Although your private school is not accredited, you can offer a high school diploma. Diplomas and covers can be purchased from school supply stores, textbook publishers, or HSLDA. Some families choose to custom-make their own diplomas using a desktop publishing program. Be sure to include the graduation date on the diploma and also to list it on your student's transcript.

CHSPE and GED

The California High School Proficiency Exam (CHSPE) and General Education Diploma (GED) both provide to those who pass the exam a certificate which is used in place of or in addition to high school diplomas.

Successful completion of the CHSPE results in a "Certificate of Proficiency," which is equivalent to a high school diploma, and is accepted by California's colleges which require a high school diploma (though it may not satisfy specific prerequisite course requirements). This exam is open to any person 16 years or older, or any person who has been enrolled in the 10th grade for one academic year or longer, or who will complete one academic year of 10th grade at the end of the semester during which the exam will be conducted. Examinations are usually held once in the fall semester and once in the spring. The current test schedule, registration form, and information about the CHSPE is available on the Internet at www.chspe.net.

The GED is a national test designed for older students who have not completed high school. Students are eligible to take the GED if they will be 18 or older on the day of the test, or if they are within 60 days of turning 18 on the day of the test. Certain exceptions are available for 17-year-olds. A GED certificate is issued upon passing, and it is generally accepted in place of a high school diploma by colleges or employers who require one.

College Admission

Can a homeschooled student go to college? The simple answer is yes. Many colleges and universities now have recruitment programs specifically to attract homeschool graduates.

For college admission, the key is to check the admission requirements for the college your student wants to attend well in advance of admissions deadlines. You would hate to find out too late that your student needs a particular course during high school in order to be eligible. For example, many four-year colleges require that students take two years of the same foreign language in high school.

Most four-year colleges require students to take the SAT or ACT exams. Information on the exams, recommendations for when to take them, preparation materials, and registration forms are available online. The SAT information is at www.collegeboard.com, and the ACT information is at www.act.org.

Since the College Board also has a lot of good information about high school courses and preparing for college, you may want to visit it at the beginning of your planning for high school just to peruse the many ideas there.

When your student submits an application for college, you will usually need to send a copy of his high school transcript. A transcript is a record of courses taken in high school, grades, and other school-related information. You can make your own transcript easily on your computer, but keep it professional-looking by following one of the formats shown in our samples in the appendix. For complete information about keeping high school records, see *The High School Handbook*.

Scholarships

Many parents wonder whether homeschooling through high school means their children will not be able to get scholarships for college. The truth is that many scholarships are available regardless of where students go to high school. While there are entire books written on applying for scholarships, a good start is to review the scholarship information presented by The College Board, www.collegeboard.com. This is the same organization that offers the SAT and PSAT exams.

Many scholarships rely on the scores students earn on the PSAT exam. This exam is taken by 11th grade students and is used for determination of National Merit Scholars, as well as for many scholarships. To prepare for the exam, check out the College Board website at least by the middle of 10th grade.

CHEA offers a $1,000 scholarship for college or vocational school each year through its Support Network, which is a branch of the ministry devoted to serving leaders of California homeschool groups. Each Support Network group leader may nominate two students whose parents are CHEA Members. For more information, ask your CHEA Support Network group leader for an application.

Special Needs

Learning Disabilities

Special needs. Learning disabilities. Learning differences. All labels that many home educating families desire to avoid. When a group of homeschooling parents was asked, "Does your child have special needs?" One parent responded, "Yes. All my children are special and they all have needs." This response is absolutely true. Then just what are educational special needs?

The education world is full of initials and buzz words: IEP, ADHD, LD, dyslexia, dysgraphia, auditory impairment, and so on. If your child has been in a classroom situation, you may have heard these terms and felt not just confused but unable to adequately prepare your child for adulthood. HSLDA uses this definition that seems to help parents decide whether their child fits what is commonly called "special needs:"

- a child who is working two or more years behind grade level in the majority of his subjects, or

- a child who has been receiving special education services, or

- a child with any other disability that seriously affects the ability to learn.

Of course, your homeschooled child may have never been in a classroom or had a "diagnosis." Your child may be a special needs child if learning is difficult or, at least, not done in a manner we are used to. The beauty of homeschooling is that no matter what type of learner your child is, you will be able to accommodate any special needs.

Little research has been done in this area of homeschooling. One reason may be is that home educating parents often don't single-out or label their child who has learning differences. One interesting statistic shows that students learning in the home are involved in "academic engaged time (AET)" 59% of the time compared to 22% of the time for public-school students. With this kind of attention to academics, it is no wonder that, when compared to special education programs, homeschools provide equal if not more advantages for special needs children. (Brian Ray, Ph.D., *Homeschooling on the Threshold, A Survey of Research At the Dawn of the New Millennium*. NHERI Publications: www.nheri.com, 1999.)

Some notions that are ingrained in education circles are "grade level," the need to know all subjects and do all tasks equally well, and even that learning requires being able to sit still. Often a child is labeled as having learning disabilities simply because these notions do not fit, or because the method of teaching is not compatible with the child's method of learning. Many special needs children who are brought home from traditional school quickly "catch up" because their individual learning needs are met.

As with many areas of homeschooling, misinformation abounds. Most troubling for many parents is the Individual Education Plan (IEP). In public schools, IEPs are developed by a group of interested people: teacher, specialist, counselor, and parent. It is a plan that includes educational goals for the child, steps for reaching each of those goals, and each interested person's role in achieving the goal. The IEP will also include any necessary assessment tools as well as resources such as speech therapy or special transportation needs.

Contrary to what some parents have been told, an IEP is not necessary after your child is removed from a public school. Some services, such as speech therapy, may be discontinued; although the Individuals with Disabilities Education Act (IDEA) requires public school districts provide services to private school students who both need and want to participate in them. Because of the potential conflict with well-meaning resource people and school personnel, it is recommended that you seek any needed services through private sources rather than through the public schools.

It is legal to homeschool your learning-disabled child, just as it is legal to homeschool any other child. You do not need special permission from the public school or other agencies. Your right to homeschool remains the same whether your child has been diagnosed with a special problem or not.

Public schools do not like to lose children enrolled in special programs, both because special and additional funding is received by the district for each student enrolled in those programs, and because special needs teachers often feel they are better able to work with your child because of their special training. But the same advantages that homeschooling offers to other children are especially applicable to those with special needs.

What better way to individualize your child's education than the one-on-one attention you can provide. Even with aides, specialists, and an IEP, your child will not receive such individual lesson plans and tutoring in a classroom setting. As the parent, you are more intimately aware of your child's individual needs than a team of professionals, and you are able to provide for those needs.

Other Disabilities

In addition to learning disabilities, many children excel in the homeschool setting despite severe challenges. Children with Down Syndrome, blindness, deafness, debilitating illnesses, paralysis, and many other disabilities seem to thrive at home. Again, the one-on-one attention, the depth of love and care of a parent, the individualized school program, the closeness with siblings, and more, all work to provide a top education. Of course, if your child has a disability, you may want special resources to help teach him.

Addressing each potential area of special needs is beyond the scope of this book, but there is help available. Some resources are included in the appendix, and others are available online at CHEA's website: www.cheaofca.org.

Gifted and Talented

As Christians, talking about our children's gifts often means the unique spiritual gifts that God gives every believer. Too often Christian parents who are teaching children with special abilities feel that they cannot or should not think about their child as being specially gifted. After all, all people are gifted by God for His purposes.

The fact is some people's talents and abilities don't fit the norms of our society. Children with these special abilities are different. These children don't relate to other people the same way, don't learn the same way, and don't perceive life the same way. These differences call for different ways of teaching.

There was a time in the education world that "gifted" meant only those with superior intelligence or a high score on an IQ test. More recently, there has been a realization that gifts may be in areas other than intelligence. The child artist, the ten-year-old graduating from college, or even the exceptional athlete are all gifted and talented.

Parents with gifted and talented children have the same questions as other parents but from a different perspective. If a child is especially talented in math, for example, parents may question if they are capable of teaching him. Families who live in rural areas may be concerned about nurturing talents that require special tutoring. Because the social needs of a highly intelligent child are different than for other children, parents may wonder if the local homeschool group can accommodate those needs.

Like special needs, this is another area that has had little research done. Part of the reason is that few home-educating parents admit they have gifted and talented children. Not to mention that some in the homeschool community wrongly judge parents of gifted children as prideful. Actually, having a gifted child has nothing to do with pride; gifted children aren't *better* than others, they just learn differently. Maybe to other parents it doesn't matter if your child is gifted, but it does to you. You want to be sure that you provide the best educational fit, in the same way you want to make sure your child's shoes fit properly.

Like parents of special needs children, parents of gifted children wonder if they are up to the task. You are. As a parent, you are able to see your child as a whole, rather than just the special ability. It is your ability to give individual attention that makes it possible for you to nurture your child's strengths while helping in the areas of weakness. You will be able to raise a confident, well-educated child who will grow to an adult who serves God.

Gifted children can become intensely interested in one subject and may pursue it with an obsession. Since you are not limited by an artificial schedule, you can vary the schedule and course work to accommodate your child's passion.

Sometimes a gifted child is years ahead in one academic area and behind in another. Rather than being confined to a traditional course of study that requires all subjects be taught at the same level, your gifted child can read seventh-grade books and work in a third-grade math book, while pursuing high school level history. It is not unusual for a gifted child to also have learning disabilities masking the gifted potential. Again, many of these complications have been overcome by the individualized education that homeschooling provides.

As with homeschooling in general, you don't have to be proficient in all areas to successfully teach your gifted child. Where you need help, homeschool groups often have other parents who can provide tips, resources, and even tutoring in specialized areas or small group classes. Sometimes local private schools will allow homeschooled students to enroll in one or two classes. Local colleges may allow high school students to take a few classes. And don't overlook the valuable resources in your community. There are likely hobby clubs, businesses, associations, libraries with information and study materials that can help.

Because gifted children can be very passionate, almost obsessive, about their current interest, their intensity can confuse parents and annoy other children. A very intelligent child can be perceived as obnoxious, even to adults. More important than academics, it is vital that you teach your special child manners and consideration for others. No matter the gift or talent, character comes first. The fact that most homeschooled students spend time with a wide age range of people helps with the social maturity needed.

Whatever gift your child has been given, training children to use their gift for the glory of God is a Christian parent's primary responsibility.

Resources for Gifted and Talented Children

There are few resources specifically for homeschooling the gifted child, so you will become your child's best advocate as you seek stimulating and appropriate education resources. Here are some ideas to help the gifted child:

- Find a Mentor. Many senior citizens are happy to share their knowledge with an interested child no matter the age. Ask around your church or community senior center. Small businesses will often allow a well-behaved student to watch or even take part in some of the business activities.

- Local Library. If your seven-year-old is reading on a junior high level, the popular books may be inappropriate. Ask your librarian for recommendations of reading material for your child.

- Special Interest Clubs. Some community special interest groups welcome children. They are happy to help nurture a shared interest. Look for astronomy clubs, birding clubs, train clubs — the possibilities are endless. Special interest might also be investigated through a scouting or 4-H program.

- Community Classes. Organizations such as historical societies or art associations often offer classes for a nominal fee or free of charge on specific topics that can provide the stimulation your gifted child needs.

- College Courses. In addition to regular academic classes, many colleges offer classes on specific subjects such as photography, journal writing, or website design. These are usually short-term and don't have the same restrictions that academic classes might.

With some classes and organizations, you may need to convince the organizers that your nine-year-old can handle the situation. Here are some ways to deal with these issues:

- Call and ask to talk to the organizer or teacher personally. Sometimes the problem is that the person taking enrollment doesn't have the authority to deviate from the usual rules.

- Ask for a trial. With a reluctant leader, suggest a trial period. Make sure the trial is more than one class for your child to overcome any shyness or to get used to a group situation.

- Offer to attend with your child. In homeschool groups it is not unusual for parents to be required to attend classes with their children. In other settings, it is quite out of the ordinary. So if the leader is reluctant to have you attend the group, offer to sit outside in case you are needed.

- Just go. Some parents are comfortable enrolling their children in spite of age requirements. When they show up for the first class, they attend as though it is perfectly normal. This is not usually the recommended way to have your gifted child included in activities outside his age group, but sometimes it works.

Chapter Six

Social Issues
and Outings

Homeschool Groups

You will find lots of different kinds of homeschool groups. While each group is as different as the families who belong, there are some basic types.

A PSP is a private school which serves homeschoolers by enrolling homeschool students. Most PSPs offer a variety of group activities, but your students must usually be enrolled and pay tuition in order to participate. The PSP usually exists to offer enrollment to homeschoolers, to keep school records, and to offer support services and activities.

In support groups, the members either have set up their own private schools in their homes (filing their own affidavits) or they belong to a PSP. The support group usually exists to offer support services and activities but does not enroll your student in a school and does not keep school records.

A third type of group is a co-op. A co-op is a homeschool group in which parents work together to educate their children, usually by taking turns teaching classes. A co-op may offer school enrollment (like a PSP) along with school records. It also may offer may other kinds of activities besides group classes.

Finally, a fourth type of group is a "special interest" group. This is a group which is set up with one focus, for example a debate group or a sports group. As you can imagine, the kinds of special interest groups are endless. Typically they don't offer school enrollment or activities like a PSP or support group does.

Increasingly you will find groups that operate exclusively in cyberspace. These virtual groups can be any one of the four types listed. Or, in some areas, the virtual group is simply an email list that announces upcoming events. Like those which meet in-person, cyber-groups vary greatly in structure and opportunities.

Even with these four general categories of groups, remember that the group you join may fit somewhere between the categories. The key to finding the group that is right for you is a lot like finding a home church. Know what you believe and what you're looking for, ask a lot of questions, visit a few times before you join, and pray for God's direction on where you will be able to serve Him and where your family will find friends and a home.

What Can You Expect?

Common activities offered by homeschool groups include all the things you thought your children might miss out on by being homeschooled: science fairs, sports teams, spelling bees, field trips, special assembly programs, reading clubs, and more. Because of the unique nature of homeschooling, the "PTA" will probably be a lot more active.

Homeschool parents need encouragement, friends, and opportunities to swap tips, cautions, success stories, and even a few horror stories. Parent meetings and Moms' Nights Outs are common. Park days are the original homeschool group mainstay, and lots of groups still offer them. The sky is the limit in activities, literally — some groups have built model rockets and launched them to the heavens.

Many homeschool groups publish newsletters with important information for the local area. Some groups print their newsletter and mail it the old-fashioned way, while others have moved to an online version.

Finding a Homeschool Group

When you're looking for a local homeschool group, the following questions should help you pinpoint what you're looking for, as well as what the group is looking for. Hopefully you'll both find a good match:

1. Is the group a PSP, a support group, a co-op, or a special interest group?
2. Does the group have any written information available that they will send to you to read at your leisure, such as a statement of faith, statement of purpose, by-laws, sample newsletter, brochure, application, etc.?
3. What are the requirements for membership? Specifically, ask about:
    - time commitment (Must you host meetings, organize activities, etc.?)
    - spiritual commitment (Is there a statement of faith; if so, must you sign it?)
    - educational commitment (Must you teach your children a particular way or use a particular curriculum?)
    - financial commitment (How much are dues, tuition, and other fees?)
4. Is there a particular philosophy espoused by the group? Denominational, educational, etc.?
5. How is the group run?
    - Is there a single leader or a board? If there is a board, are board members elected or appointed?
    - Is it operated as an income-producing business or as a community co-op? If a business, what services do you receive for your payment? If a co-op, what responsibilities will you have as a member?
    - How are the members involved in decisions?
6. What are the fathers' roles in the group? Are the dads involved at all? Are they required to be? What percent of fathers participate in group activities?
7. Is the group leader a member of CHEA's Support Network? You'll want to make sure the group has access to up-to-date legal and legislative information, as well as events happening around the state.
8. What are the ages of the children who attend the group's activities? For example, if there are 10-15 field trips planned each

year, how many are geared to teens and how many to early elementary grades?

9. What are the routine activities scheduled? Many groups offer exciting yearly events like science fairs, spelling bees, etc. But it is at the regular, on-going activities that you will likely form lasting friendships. Common activities are park days, field trips, parents meetings, and groups classes. Ask about the days and times these activities take place.

10. Are there group classes for children? Is attendance at such classes mandatory? If you are interested in participating in group classes, ask who the teachers are, whether the teachers are Christians, what the class topics are, what materials are used in teaching, what the parents' involvement in children's classes is, and what the cost is.

11. Are there classes or meetings for parents? Is attendance at such meetings mandatory? If mandatory, how often must you attend and what happens if you are absent? Who are the speakers and what are the topics? What is the schedule and cost?

12. Does the group require copies of any school records or pupil records from its member families? Most support groups don't; most PSPs do. Check elsewhere in this manual to see what records are required by law. Make sure a PSP requires these, but also feel free to ask why they require any additional items. Make sure a support group has experienced leaders who can help you if you have questions with records.

13. For a PSP, also ask:
    - Is there a school-wide course of study, or do families submit their own?
    - How are high school credits awarded and what is required for graduation from high school?
    - Is standardized testing required, and, if so, what ages must be tested?
    - Are there extra fees for activities, testing, registration, etc.?

While many homeschoolers manage without joining any group at all, the encouragement and edification you'll find make it a strong recommendation that you find one and become an active member. Even if you don't feel you need encouragement, someone else needs your support. This also applies to families who have only preschoolers now, but are interested in or already committed to home education.

You can find a variety of homeschool groups at the CHEA website, www.cheaofca.org, in the Homeschool Directory. Remember that the group you join will only be as good as you and the other members make it. While it's impossible to find a perfect group, it's realistic to expect to find a group that meets your needs, makes you feel welcome, fosters good friendships, and allows you to use your gifts and talents to serve others.

In addition to finding a local group, you should join CHEA, the only statewide Christian organization for homeschoolers in California. CHEA's mission is to promote, support, and defend private home education in California. CHEA works with local support groups for mutual benefit, gives counsel on all matters concerning home education, provides resource information, works with educators, lawyers, courts and legislators, and publishes a digital magazine. Even if you're not a Member, you're benefitting from the work CHEA has done for more than 30 years. Membership is reasonably priced and will ensure that good work continues.

CHEA Members also get a discount on Convention registration fees and on all books and materials sold by CHEA, and on HSLDA membership. There are no requirements for Membership other than paying the annual dues. To become a CHEA Member, call CHEA at 562-864-2432, or visit the CHEA website (www.cheaofca.org).

Field Trips

One common charge against home educators is that they are isolated and out of touch with the real world. Nothing could be further from the truth. Homeschooling families, through their homeschool groups or individually, can provide more real world opportunities than many traditional schools can.

For homeschoolers, even typical errands around town become field trips as children learn to shop, do the banking, and handle a variety of similar tasks with their parents. Homeschool groups offer opportunities for group rates to popular attractions such as the community theater. Large venues, such as Magic Mountain or local water parks, may even offer special homeschool days with attractive family prices.

An individual family or a few families can go to many of the familiar field trip locations. For elementary age children or younger, behind-the-scenes visits to post offices, grocery stores, fire stations, and other interesting businesses and service providers are common and easily planned. Generally it takes just one phone call to set up a special visit. All ages can attend together, and just three or four families will make a nice size group.

For older children, local museums, galleries, and less-familiar businesses make good field trips. Some museums and galleries require a minimum number of students. Others allow students to attend free with a nominal charge for parents. Look through the community pages of the phone book, the yellow pages, or online, and you'll find lots of ideas. Better yet, let your older students look and choose a couple of places they would like to visit.

Evaluating Activities

Especially at the beginning of a new school year, it is easy to become involved in the busyness of many activities, field trips, classes, and educational opportunities. By asking yourself the following questions, you can evaluate each opportunity to ensure that it fits with your priorities and will help keep your homeschooling consistent:

1. What will this activity cost us in family time, energy, and finances?

2. Will this opportunity draw our family closer to the Lord and to each other, or will it separate us?

3. Will this activity hinder our local church attendance or ministry?

4. Will this class educate or entertain?

5. Will this activity help meet one of our family's top priorities?

6. Will this activity cause our family to feel stress or bless?

7. Will this opportunity teach us a skill that makes us better servants of God?

8. Will this opportunity unnecessarily take us away from home?

Homeschool Etiquette

As Christian homeschoolers it is important to represent the Lord and the homeschool community well. This means modeling and teaching your children proper behavior—etiquette, if you will. When others see an ill-mannered child they are likely to conclude homeschooling is not working.

Academic proficiency should be strengthened by good manners, which come out of Christian love for others, sincerity, a desire not to offend, and self-control. In other words, demonstrate godly character.

While you always want to strive for mannerly behavior, there are a few places to be particularly careful. For example, when participating in field trips and other outings, children and adults should arrive on time and be courteous. Although it requires consistency and supervision, it is not hard to teach your children to open doors, shake hands when introduced, maintain eye contact, listen quietly, and remember to say "Please" and "Thank you." These small acts make huge impressions.

Table manners, addressing people properly, greeting people as they enter your home, exercising hospitality, and proper conduct in church and all public places are important lessons to be taught to your children, and, of course, modeled by you. Many families incorporate teaching of manners into their daily school routine by choosing a topic or two to discuss during Bible time. Some families do this as a separate "course," for a set period of time, while others choose one day each week to talk about this important topic. Whatever method you choose to teach etiquette, plan to teach it each year as it is one of those areas that needs constant work to develop a lifelong habit.

When answering the telephone, children should answer properly and courteously with a greeting such as, "Hello, Smith Residence. May I ask who is calling?" Children should be taught what information they should give to callers. For example, children should never tell callers the parents are not at home; instead they should say the parent is not available to take the phone call right now. A child who is not able to write down an accurate message should not be allowed to answer the phone if you are not available. Of course, you will teach your younger children how to answer, but they should do so only when you are right there with them.

It is wise not to allow children to answer the telephone during school hours. In fact, many homeschoolers think it is wise for *you* to avoid answering the phone during school hours. Those "quick" calls can eat up your school schedule before you know it. Instead, let your machine handle calls while you teach, then return them after school so that you can focus on your new full-time job: teaching

Chapter Seven

Other Questions and Challenges

School Building Safety Issues

Asbestos Hazard Requirements

After filing an affidavit, you may receive letters concerning asbestos hazard requirements. According to the General Services Office (GSO) of Local Assistance staff, the Asbestos Hazard Emergency Response Act (AHERA) does not apply to private schools conducted in private family residences. The AHERA is aimed at older school buildings where students meet for regular classes.

In any case, the GSO is not a compliance agency, only an assistance agency. The compliance agency in this matter is the Environmental Protection Agency, which has stated that it will not require parents who educate their children at home to comply with the AHERA.

While you should keep any letters you receive about this matter on file, you don't need to respond unless you are conducting classes on a daily basis in a public building with other families' children.

Earthquake Emergency Procedures

California state law requires each school, public and private, which has 50 or more students enrolled or has more than one classroom, to establish an earthquake emergency procedure system. (E.C. §§ 35295, 35296, and 35297) Most homeschools have fewer than 50 students and less than two classrooms, so the earthquake emergency procedure requirement does not apply. These regulations are intended to ensure that public buildings and those inside them are safe during earthquakes. Private residences are subject to different building and safety codes than buildings used primarily as schools.

Fire and Health Department Building Inspections

Fire and health department building inspections also do not apply to homeschools, because the primary use of the "school building" is as a residence.

Surveys and Reports in the Mail

Other Reports, Surveys and Programs

Each year private schools receive various surveys in the mail or by phone. For example many received the "Status of HIV Prevention Education in California" and the "Private School Universe Survey" from the United States Census Bureau. Unless law mandates a response, you simply do not have to respond.

Other than filing an affidavit each year, the only reports that you are required to complete and return are those covered in the section on "School Health Reports."

Various federal and state programs are often made available to private schools. You may respectfully decline to participate.

Contact from Public School Officials or Social Services

Contact From Public School Officials

Establishing a home-based private school is legal, but occasionally a school district tries to investigate homeschoolers. Some homeschool families have received requests for information from their school district superintendents or attendance officers. Usually these requests have been for such items as attendance records, curriculum, teacher qualifications, schedules, business licenses, school policies, list of all enrolled students, or similar items. However, unless they have a warrant or a court order, counties and school districts do not have the legal authority to go beyond simply verifying that a student is in regular attendance at your school, and that your school has filed the annual private school affidavit.

If a public school official contacts you, be courteous and professional. If they ask about a specific student whose name they already have, you can confirm whether that student is enrolled and in regular attendance in a private school. If they ask about students in general without giving you a name, then politely tell them that the identity of students is confidential information. If they contact you to ask about school information, everything you are required to disclose is already on the private school affidavit. Since that is a public document, feel free to confirm any information on it. You can even offer to send them a copy, although they should have access to the information already.

HSLDA members should call HSLDA any time public officials contact them about their homeschooling. This helps us to track what is happening around the state and determine whether a contact is an isolated incident or a larger issue.

Social Services Contacts

Sometimes a well-meaning, yet uninformed neighbor or relative will contact authorities to report that a child is not attending school. Sometimes a homeschool family may be contacted by Child Protective Services (CPS) or other authorities because of these reports. HSLDA recommends that each family have a planned response to these kinds of contacts. This way, you will not be caught off guard and will be able to handle the contact calmly and professionally.

Consider the following guidelines:

1. You generally do not have to let anyone into your house unless the person has a search warrant. In some situations, a social worker may arrive with a police officer, which can indicate their intent to enter the home. However, even when a police officer is present, a search warrant is required unless it appears to the officer that the children may be in danger.

   Thus, if there is no police officer present, you can tell social workers you will not allow them to enter. They may cajole or threaten to come back with the police, but if you remain firm in your denial of permission, they cannot enter. Even if they call the police to assist them, you will have time to contact HSLDA and ask for help.

   If there *is* a police officer present, he or she may ask for permission to come in. If you deny permission, the officer will have to make a determination of whether the circumstances indicate that a warrant is not needed. If the officer says he or she will enter despite your denial of permission, you should comply with the officer's demands and let them in—it's either stepping aside or risking arrest. But politely tell them again that the entry is without your permission.

2. Whether the social worker is alone or accompanied by police, ask for identification of each person present. Get each person's name, agency's name, and telephone number. Take business cards or write the information down.

3. Ask what the complaints or allegations are. Under California law, if you are the subject of an investigation of child abuse or neglect, you must be advised of what the complaints or allegations are when you are contacted by Child Protective Services workers. However, do not expect to be told who made the complaint; this information is confidential.

4. If you are an HSLDA member, contact them immediately. They may be able to intervene while the social worker is at the door. On at least one occasion, HSLDA was able to resolve the matter by having the phone taken to the CPS worker outside the member's door.

5. If the contact is via telephone, write down the person's name, agency's name, telephone number, nature of the call. Also ask what the complaint or allegation is. Set up a time to call the person back. Then call HSLDA for guidance in how to respond.

While these suggestions will not apply in all situations, they do provide general guidelines. It may be that you will be able to resolve the matter with an explanation that your family is legally homeschooling pursuant to the private school law in the State of California.

If You Need Legal Help

We hope you never need legal help related to homeschooling, but each year many families do. Whether you're contacted by CPS investigating truancy, just have a legal question, or actually end up in court over homeschooling, you'll find a membership in the Home School Legal Defense Association to be invaluable.

Some parents feel if they are not imminently threatened then they don't need to spend money on association membership. But what happens to one, in a very real sense, affects all. And even though we have good laws in place now, challenges pop up quickly.

The legal arguments in a constitutional issue such as home education are so complicated that it would be foolhardy for a family to go into court without an attorney. Good lawyers can cost

> ### John Adams' View on Obeying Authorities
>
> It is interesting to note the guiding principles of the colonists on the eve of the War of Independence. According to John Adams, these principles came from the most influential book in America at that time, *Vindiciae Contra Tyrranos* (written in 1579, author unknown).
>
> These principles were:
>
> 1) The ruler cannot command anything contrary to the Law of God. Any ruler who does so seeks to be like God and forfeits his right to the obedience of his subjects.
>
> 2) Rebellion is properly defined as a refusal to obey God. To obey the unlawful commands of a ruler is rebellion against God.
>
> 3) Resistance against a tyrannical ruler is obedience to God when the ruler is in conflict with God's laws.

thousands of dollars. And finding one who specializes in home education issues can be difficult. Just one isolated negative case can set a terrible precedent for everyone, so it's important to have good legal help widely available. For these reasons, HSLDA was established in 1983. Since then, HSLDA has offered outstanding service to homeschoolers across the U.S. and around the world.

Other legal associations besides HSLDA have popped up, some with lower prices, some operating by donation only. Yet CHEA continues to recommend that all homeschool families join HSLDA. Why?

Consider these facts and compare them to any other legal representation you are considering:

HSLDA is staffed by full-time Christian attorneys who specialize in home education freedoms. Some other organizations use non-attorneys to handle preliminary legal work and contacts. But in our legal system, attorneys are given far more access and credence than non-attorneys. Additionally, non-attorneys simply do not have the training nor legal expertise to handle every legal issue that arises, and sometimes they arise during preliminary conversations and meetings.

HSLDA attorneys will not only represent you in court, but will talk with you, and will handle administrative issues when necessary, such as making phone calls or writing letters to authorities in your behalf. In short, they'll provide you with legal services even when you're not being taken to court. Additionally, HSLDA will work to keep you out of court rather than waiting until a hearing or a court date has been set.

If you're an HSLDA member, you're guaranteed help. Some organizations depend upon the availability of volunteer attorneys, which means there's no guarantee your case will be accepted.

HSLDA has more than 25 years of experience. They have successfully handled thousands of legal issues related to homeschooling.

For more information and a membership application:
HSLDA
P.O. Box 3000
Purcellville, VA 20134
540-338-5600
info@hslda.org

Will the Laws Change?

Laws do change. In fact, new laws are proposed so often in California that in the 1980's a full-time legislative consultant was needed just to monitor all the legislative bills. Thousands of bills pass through our legislature every year, and Roy Hanson and Nathan Pierce of Family Protection Ministries all work full-time now in watching out for homeschoolers when it comes to legislation.

In addition to monitoring bills for specific effect on homeschoolers, FPM's staff also works to protect parental rights on a much broader scope. They coordinate with other homeschool, educational, and family organizations as needed to provide a concerted effort when needed to defeat bad legislation or champion good.

FPM is fully supported by donations and prayers. Those who donate at least $40 per year receive Roy's newsletter, *The Private/Home Educators of California Legal-Legislative Update*.

To contribute or for further information, contact:

Family Protection Ministries

P.O. Box 730

Lincoln, CA 95648-0730

www.pheofca.org

Appendix A

Resources

Recommended Reading

The following books are recommended for a good, general understanding of why families are turning to home education and the various aspects involved, from the theoretical and philosophical to the practical.

This list cannot be, and is not intended to be, exhaustive; there are many, many books on home education and more are being published all the time. This list does represent a cross sampling of the best available. These books also represent a variety of philosophies. It is important to read several books on home education and use your own God-given discernment in balancing the various positions. Please note, neither the authors nor CHEA of California agree with every point presented in every book listed.

100 Top Picks for Homeschool Curriculum: Choosing the Right Curriculum and Approach for Your Child's Learning Style
Cathy Duffy
(2005, B&H Publishing Group, ISBN 0805431381)

Help for choosing curriculum by understanding your own educational philosophy, your child's learning style, and looking at which curriculum will be a right fit. Covers every subject area.

The Basic Steps to Successful Homeschooling

Vicki A. Brady

(1996, Vital Issues Press, ISBN 1 563841134)

A practical, nuts and bolts approach to Christian homeschooling.

Beyond Survival: A Guide to Abundant-Life Homeschooling

Diana Waring

(1996, Emerald Books, ISBN 1883002370)

A practical guide to Christian homeschooling which helps parents prepare and develop a working plan.

A Biblical Home Education: Building Your Homeschool on the Foundation of God's Word

Ruth Beechick

(2007, B&H Publishing Group, ISBN 0805444548)

Dr. Beechick is a respected leader in the homeschool movement. In this book, she teaches homeschoolers to focus all their teaching on God's Word.

A Biblical Psychology of Learning: How Your Mind Works

Ruth Beechick

(1982, Accent Publications, ISBN 0896360830)

Don't let the title scare you; this book is very readable. Discusses various psychological approaches to learning and presents a biblical alternative learning model that includes our "spiritual being." Offers practical teaching methods.

CHEA's Firm Foundation Library

A collection of books at a package-deal price to help home-educating parents integrate biblical principles throughout the curriculum so that children and parents develop a consistent, comprehensive Christian worldview. Includes:

Homeschooling from a Biblical Worldview, by Israel Wayne
Homeschooling: The Right Choice by Christopher Klicka
Let Us Highly Resolve, by David and Shirley Quine, and
Encyclopedia of Bible Truths, by Ruth Haycock.

The Christian Home School
Gregg Harris
(1988, Wolgemuth and Hyatt, ISBN 094349706X)

An in-depth look at the principles (biblical, historical, practical) behind home education. A very thorough book by a well-respected national home education leader.

A Christian Manifesto
Dr. Francis Schaeffer
(2005, Crossway Books, ISBN 1581346921)

Shows how the whole foundation for society has shifted radically from its original Judeo-Christian basis to a humanistic basis. It calls for action in government, law, and all of life to turn the tide of moral decadence and loss of freedom. Other books written by members of the Schaeffer family are also highly recommended.

Encyclopedia of Bible Truths
Ruth Haycock
(1993, Association of Christian Schools International, ASIN B001PPXFK6)

A comprehensive look at every school subject and what the Bible principles are that govern it.

For the Children's Sake: Foundations of Education for Home and School
Susan Schaeffer Macaulay
(1984, Crossway Books, ISBN 089107290X)

Must reading for parents who desire to give their children a true education by awakening their minds and giving them richness, stability, and joy for living.

Gaining Confidence to Teach: Forty-Two Confidence-Builders to Encourage Christian Homeschoolers
Debbie Strayer
(1997, Common Sense Press, ISBN 1880892987)

Encouragement for homeschoolers to rely on God and His faithfulness to confidently homeschool.

Going Home to School (Why So Many Christians Are)
Llewellyn B. Davis
(1991, The Elijah Company, ISBN 1884098002)

One of the most readable and thorough books explaining the reasons behind the philosophy of Christian home education.

A Guide to American Christian Education for the Home and School: The Principle Approach
James Rose
(2002, Providence Foundation, ISBN 0961620110)

Teaches the rudiments of The Principle Approach philosophy of education, discusses the role of the home in education, how to develop a curriculum compatible with this philosophy, and shares examples of courses designed for this approach. This book will challenge you to a biblical, Christian view of education and history.

The High School Handbook: For Junior High, Too
Mary Schofield
(2004, Christian Home Educators Press, ISBN 0966093771)

Offers help in homeschooling junior and senior high school students by providing information about educational goals, graduation, course descriptions, college admissions, transcripts, reading suggestions for teens, and more.

Home Educating with Confidence
Rick & Marilyn Boyer
(1996, The Learning Parent, ISBN 0970877056)

An encouraging book by parents who began homeschooling their fourteen children in 1980. Common sense tips with good-natured humor.

The Home School Manual: Plans, Pointers, Reasons, and Resources
Theodore Wade
(1986, Gazelle Publications, ISBN 0930192362)

Covers just about every aspect of homeschooling, especially for parents of older children, but does touch upon early vs. later academics.

Homeschooling from a Biblical Worldview
Israel Wayne
(2000, Wisdom's Gate, ISBN 0615113656)

An excellent tool for learning how every subject teaches of God's nature and character. Helps parents learn to think biblically and teach their children to do the same.

Home Schooling: The Right Choice: An Academic, Historical, Practical, and Legal Perspective
Christopher J. Klicka
(2001, B&H Publishing Group, ISBN 0805425853)

This is THE book about Christian educational philosophy and contains practical aspects as well.

Honey for a Child's Heart
Gladys Hunt
(2002, Zondervan, ISBN 0310242460)

A beautiful book on reading, selecting good books, and the place books should have in your family, including an extensive bibliography of great books for different age levels, reading ability, and interests.

The How and Why of Homeschooling
Ray E. Ballman
(1987, Crossway Books, ISBN 0891078592)

An excellent first book to be read by the person interested in Christian home education. Unique to this book is an encouraging chapter for grandparents.

The Hurried Child
David Elkind
(2006, Da Capo Press, ISBN 073821082X)

A good commentary on our culture's tendency to rush our children into the adult world. It has chapters on parents, schools, and media (secular orientation).

Is Public Education Necessary?
Samuel Blumenfeld
(1987, Devin-Adair Publishers, ISBN 0941995046)

An excellent history of public education showing how it evolved to the modern day. It is a sobering account of the reasons behind public schools and goals of those who promote them.

Let Us Highly Resolve: Families Living for Christ in the 21st Century

David and Shirley Quine

(1996, Cornerstone Curriculum, ISBN 0965651207)

An encouraging and challenging book on the importance of a biblical worldview and how to instill one in your children and yourself.

Philosophy of Christian Curriculum

R. J. Rushdoony

ISBN 1879998289

Ross House Books

An all-time classic of biblical education. The author shows how each subject can be taught from a biblical perspective.

Preschool at Home

Debbie Feely

(2000, Christian Home Educators Press, ISBN 0966093798)

An easy-to-read booklet on homeschooling preschool children, using an informal and practical approach to encourage children's natural and growing abilities.

Preschool: At What Cost?

Susan K. Stewart

(2011, Practical Inspirations, ISBN 978-976739429-9)

A detailed look at the studies behind the push for formal preschool programs. This book challenges the notion that young children benefit from early formal academics.

School Can Wait

Dr. Raymond S. Moore and Dorothy N. Moore

(1989, Hewitt Research Foundation, ISBN 9780842512831)

Better Late than Early: A New Approach to Your Child's Education

Dr. Raymond S. Moore and Dorothy N. Moore

(1989, Reader's Digest Association, ISBN 0842513140)

These two books were read by nearly every new homeschooler in the early years of the modern homeschool movement. Dr. Moore's research supported delayed academics and keeping children in a loving and supportive environment at home where their natural learning abilities and interests would blossom.

Shepherding a Child's Heart
Tedd Tripp
(1995, Shepherd Press, ISBN 0966378601)
Biblical approach to raising children of all ages.

Teaching to Change Lives: Seven Proven Ways to Make Your Teaching Come Alive
Howard Hendricks
(2003, Multnomah Books, ISBN 1590521382)

While not written for home educators, but rather to the Sunday School teacher and pastoral speaker, this book, nevertheless, has much to say to home educating parents on the biblical methods of teaching.

The Three R's
Ruth Beechick
(2006, Mott Media, ISBN 0880620749)

You Can Teach Your Child Successfully : Grades 4-8
Ruth Beechick
(1999, Mott Media, ISBN 0940319047)

These books will give you a solid foundation for teaching and breaking away from the clutches of too much pre-packaged curriculum.

What Are They Teaching Our Children?
Mel and Norma Gabler
(1985, Victor Books, SP Publications, ISBN 0896933660)

Documents the influence of humanism in the classroom through textbooks. If you plan to use secular texts, read this book first.

What the Bible Says about Child Training
Richard Fugate
(1996, Foundation for Biblical Research, ISBN 1889700134)

Uses biblical principles to help parents understand their God-given authority in training their children.

Will Early Education Ruin Your Child?
Richard Fugate
(1992, Alpha Omega, ASIN B000FSU3XQ)

Critiques the educational philosophy and theology of Dr. Raymond and Mrs. Dorothy Moore.

Homeschool Magazines and Newsletters

A good homeschool magazine can be a real help to your homeschooling. Regular encouragement, tips from experts and peers, new ideas, and news about what's happening in homeschool circles are all great reasons to subscribe to one or more. A few of these are available to members only, such as HSLDA's *Court Report*. CHEA's *California Parent Educator* digital magazine is free.

California Parent Educator Magazine
Christian Home Educators Association of California (CHEA)
P.O. Box 2009, Norwalk, CA 90651-2009
562-864-CHEA (2432)
cheainfo@cheaofca.org
www.cheaofca.org

California Home Educators Legal-Legislative Update
Family Protection Ministries (FPM)
P.O. Box 730, Lincoln, CA 95648-0730
916-786-3523
www.pheofca.org

The Home School Court Report
Home School Legal Defense Association (HSLDA)
P.O. Box 3000, Purcellville, VA 20134
540-338-5600
info@hslda.org
www.hslda.org

Home School Digest
Wisdom's Gate
PO Box 374, Covert, MI 49043
269-764-1910
www.homeschooldigest.com

Homeschooling Today
P.O. Box 244, Abington, VA 24212
866-804-4HST
276-628-1686
www.homeschooltoday.com

Practical Homeschooling
Home Life, Inc.
P.O. Box 1190, Fenton, MO 63026-1190
www.home-school.com

The Teaching Home Magazine
P.O. Box 20219, Portland, OR 97294-0219
503-253-9633
tth@teachinghome.com
www.teachinghome.com

Curriculum Resources

Order lots of catalogs and browse what's available before you buy. You can see thousands of items in person each year at CHEA Conventions, so a good plan would be to browse through catalogs, mark those items you'd like to see, and arrive at the Convention with a list of things to review.

Please note that there are new curriculum suppliers popping up all the time, so our list is out of date almost as fast as we print it. Check CHEA's Homeschool Directory for new entries and for direct links to many companies' websites. Also note that we can't recommend every product or service included on our list, so use your discretion when ordering.

Resource Codes

C	Classical	T	Testing Service
DL	Distance Learning, Online, or Correspondence School	TB	Text Books
		UB	Used Books
G	General Supplies and Variety of Curriculum	UN	Unschooling
		US	Unit Study
SB	Specialized Books	WT	Work Texts
SN	Special Needs		

A Beka [TB]
P.O. Box 19100, Pensacola, FL 32523-9100
877-223-5226
www.abeka.org

Academic Book Services, Inc. [UB]
200 Cook Street, Cartersville, GA 30120
800-621-4272 ext 5107
textbooks@fes.follett.com
www.academicbookservices.com

Almaden Valley Christian School [SN]
16465 Carlson Dr., Morgan Hill, CA 95037
408-776-6691
www.almadenvalleychristianschool.com

Alpha Omega Publications [WT]
804 N. 2nd Avenue, East Rock Rapids, IA 51246
800-622-3070
www.aop.com

Ambleside Online [DL]
www.amblesideonline.com

American Christian History Institute [SB]
P.O. Box 648, Palo Cedro, CA 96073
530-226-1945
jbrosebud@sbcglobal.net
www.achipa.com

American Destiny
9 Music Square South, Suite 202
Nashville, TN 37203
info@americandestiny.com
www.americandestiny.com

Association of Christian Schools International [TB, SB]
PO Box 65130, Colorado Springs, CO 80962-5130
719-528-6906
800-367-0798
customer service info@acsi.org
www.acsi.org

Association of Classical & Christian Schools [CL]
P.O. Box 9741, Moscow, ID 83843
208-882-6101
accs@turbonet.com
www.accsedu.org

Beautiful Feet Books [SB]
1306 Mill St., San Luis Obispo, CA 93401
314-721-5238
800-889-1978
letters@bfbooks.com
www.bfbooks.com

Bob Jones University Press [TB, T]
Greenville, SC 29614
800-845-5731
bjupinfo@bjupress.com
www.bjup.com

Builder Books [G]
P.O. Box 5789, Lynnwood, WA 98046
425-377-2530
800-260-5461 orders only
www.bbhomeschoolcatalog.com

Bluestocking Press [SB]
P.O. Box 1014
Placerville, CA 95667-1014
800-959-8586
530-622-8586
info@bluestockingpress.com
www.bluestockingpress.com

Resource Codes

C	Classical	T	Testing Service
DL	Distance Learning, Online, or Correspondence School	TB	Text Books
		UB	Used Books
G	General Supplies and Variety of Curriculum	UN	Unschooling
		US	Unit Study
SB	Specialized Books	WT	Work Texts
SN	Special Needs		

California High School Proficiency Exam (CHSPE) [T]
CHSPE Office Sacramento County Office of Education
P.O. Box 269003, Sacramento, CA 95826-9003
866-342-4773
chspe@scoe.net
www.chspe.net

Center for Children & Parents [SN, T]
Dr. Stanley Walters
17871 Santiago Blvd., #224, Villa Park, CA 92681
714-283-3390

Chalk Dust Company [SB]
PMB 375, 3506 Hwy 6, South Sugar Land, TX 77478-4401
800-588-7564
sales@chalkdust.com
www.chalkdust.com

Christ Centered Publications [TB]
P.O. Box 989, Sapulpa, OK 74067-0989
918-248-4301
800-778-4318
www.christcentercurriculum.com

Christian Home Educators Association of California (CHEA)
P.O. Box 2009, Norwalk, CA 90651-2009
12440 E. Firestone Bl., Ste 311, Norwalk, CA 90650
562-864-CHEA (2432)
cheainfo@cheaofca.org
www.cheaofca.org

Christian Home Educators Press [SB]
12440 E. Firestone Bl., Ste 311, Norwalk, CA 90650
562-864-2432
chep@cheaofca.org

Christian Liberty Academy School System (CLASS) [DL]
502 W. Euclid Ave., Arlington Heights, IL 60004
847-259-4444
800-832-2741 (catalog only)
custserv@homeschools.org
www.homeschools.org

Christian Light Education [WT]

P.O. Box 1212, Harrisonburg, VA 22801-1212

540-434-0750

877-226-8010

info@clp.org

www.clp.org

Common Sense Press [SB]

8786 Highway 21, Melrose, FL 32666

352-475-5757

info@cspress.com

www.cspress.com

The Cornerstone Bookstore [G]

25075 Peachland Ave., Newhall, CA 91321

805-259-4090

Creation's Child [US]

P.O. Box 3004, #44, Corvallis, OR 97339

541-758-3413

Digital Interactive Video Education [SB]

26484 El Indio Rd., Waller, TX 77484

936-372-9216

karne@diveintomath.com

www.diveintomath.com

Eagles' Nest and Christian Curriculum Cellar [G, UB]

1411 Standford Ave., Suite A, Modesto, CA 95350

209-556-9551

www.hsmarketplace.com

Resource Codes

C	Classical	T	Testing Service
DL	Distance Learning, Online, or Correspondence School	TB	Text Books
		UB	Used Books
G	General Supplies and Variety of Curriculum	UN	Unschooling
		US	Unit Study
SB	Specialized Books	WT	Work Texts
SN	Special Needs		

Escondido Tutorial Service [CL, DL]

2634 Bernardo Ave., Escondido, CA, 92029

gbt@gbt.org

www.gbt.org

Excellence in Education [G]

2640-A7 S. Myrtle Ave., Monrovia, CA 91016

626-821-0025

www.excellenceineducation.com

Family Protection Ministries (FPM)

P.O. Box 730, Lincoln, CA 95648-0730

916-786-3523

Foundation for American Christian Education (FACE) [TB, US, SB]

P.O. Box 9588, Chesapeake, VA 23121

757-488-7116

800-352-FACE

info@face.net

www.face.net

Greenleaf Press [G, SB]

3761 Hwy 109, North Lebanon, TN 37087

615-449-1617

greenleaf@softek.net

www.greenleafpress.com

GW School Supply [G]

Located in cities around California

800-234-1065

www.gwschool.com

Roy Hanson

See Family Protection Ministries

Hewitt Research Foundation [SB, T]

Hewitt Homeschooling Resources

Box 9, Washougal, WA 98671

360-835-8708

800-890-4097

info@hewitthomeschooling.com

www.hewitthomeschooling.com

Holt Associates [UN]

P. O. Box 89, Wakefield, MA 01880-5105

info@holtgws.com

www.holtgws.com

Home School Foundation

P. O. Box 1152, Purcellville, CA 20134

540-338-8688

info@homeschoolfoundation.org

www.homeschoolfoundation.org

Home School Legal Defense Association (HSLDA)

P.O. Box 3000, Purcellville, VA 20134

540-338-5600

info@hslda.org

www.hslda.org

Hope Country Schoolhouse Resource Center [G, UB]

12211 Magnolia St., Garden Grove, CA 92841

714-534-6733

info@hopecountryschoolhouse.com

www.hopecountryschoolhouse.com

Konos Character Curriculum [US]

P.O. Box 250, Anna, TX 75409

972-924-2712

info@konos.com

www.konos.com

Mott Media [TB, WT]

1130 Fenway Circle, Fenton, MI 48430

800-421-6645

www.mottmedia.com

Resource Codes

C	Classical	T	Testing Service
DL	Distance Learning, Online, or Correspondence School	TB	Text Books
		UB	Used Books
G	General Supplies and Variety of Curriculum	UN	Unschooling
		US	Unit Study
SB	Specialized Books	WT	Work Texts
SN	Special Needs		

Nadeau Educational Center [SN]
Dr. Ray Nadeau
8550 Balboa Blvd., Ste. 206, Northridge, CA 91325
818-895-8600
www.testingkit.com

National Association for Child Development [SN]
Marilee Nicoll Coots, Certified Neuroeducational Consultant
760-378-HELP (4357)
learning@kernvalley.com
www.nacd.org

**National Challenged Homeschoolers Associated Network
(NATHHAN) [SN]**
PO Box 310, Moyie Springs, ID 83845
208-267-6246
www.nathhan.com

Nature of Learning Educational Assessment Services [SN]
Marian Soderholm
562-425-7886
marian@nautreoflearning.com
www.natureoflearning.com

Nasco [G]
P. O. Box 3837, Modesto, CA 95352
800-558-9595
info@homeschool-nasco.com
www.enasco.com

Noble Institute [SB]
6920 SE Hogan Rd., Gresham OR 97080
www.nobleinstitue.org

The Plymouth Rock Foundation [SB]
1120 Long Pond Rd., Plymouth, MA 02360
800-210-1620
info@plymrock.org
www.plymrock.org

The Providence Foundation [SB]
P.O. Box 6759, Charlottesville, VA 22906
804-978-4535
info@providencefoundation.com
www.providencefoundation.com

Rod and Staff [TB]
Route 172, Crockett, KY 41413
606-522-4348

Spalding Education International [G]
2814 W. Bell Road, Suite 1405, Phoenix, AZ 85053
602-866-7801
staff@spalding.org
www.spalding.org

School of Tomorrow (ACE) [WT, T]
P.O. Box 299000, Lewisville, TX 75029-9000
972-315-1776
800-925-7777
800-873-3435 (Testing)
homeschooling@aceministries.com
www.schooloftomorrow.com

Shekinah Curriculum Cellar [G]
1815 Whittington Road, Kilgore, TX 75662
(903) 643-2760
www.shekinahcc.com

Veritas Press [DL, C]
1829 William Penn Way, Lancaster, PA 17601
800-922-5082
info@veritaspress.com
www.veritaspress.com

Weaver Curriculum [US]
See Alpha Omega
www.aop.com/weaver

Resource Codes

C	Classical	T	Testing Service
DL	Distance Learning, Online, or Correspondence School	TB	Text Books
		UB	Used Books
G	General Supplies and Variety of Curriculum	UN	Unschooling
		US	Unit Study
SB	Specialized Books	WT	Work Texts
SN	Special Needs		

Notes

World Book Educational Products [SB]
233 North Michigan Ave., Suite 2000 , Chicago, Illinois 60601
800-967-3250
www.worldbook.com

Appendix B

Información en español

Información legal básica

Educación en el hogar en California

Notas importantes: Esta hoja presenta un resumen breve del tema. Para obtener detalles e instrucciones precisas sobre cómo cumplir con todos los requisitos legales de la alternativa de escuela privada, entre los que se incluyen cómo presentar la declaración jurada de escuela privada y cómo evitar problemas legales, compre y lea detenidamente el resto de este libro. Esto deberá hacerse antes de comenzar la educación en el hogar o de retirar a su hijo/a de la escuela pública.

Las personas que tengan estudiantes de edades que corresponden a la escuela secundaria también deberán comprar y leer el *Manual de la Escuela Secundaria* de CHEA (contiene información sobre temas diversos, como por ejemplo: los requisitos para la graduación, los requisitos de los cursos de escuela secundaria, los permisos de trabajo, capacitación para los que conducen vehículos, la preparación de la educación postsecundaria, los diplomas, los registros de calificaciones de los estudiantes y exámenes como CHSPE, GED y otros).

Se podrán evitar muchos problemas legales si las personas que educan en el hogar se tomaran un tiempo para informarse mediante la lectura del material que se mencionó anteriormente. Cumplir con exigencias ilegítimas de ciertos funcionarios que van más allá de su competencia puede hacer que las cosas sean más difíciles para Usted y para otros educadores en el hogar. En la actualidad, no hay ninguna otra fuente escrita disponible que cubra los aspectos legales de la educación en el hogar en California tan exhaustiva y certeramente como los materiales de CHEA que se mencionaron anteriormente.

REQUISITOS LEGALES

A. En la actualidad no hay estatutos en vigencia en California que se ocupen específica y exclusivamente de la educación privada en el hogar.

B. Se exige que todos los estudiantes de 6 a 18 años de edad asistan obligatoriamente a escuelas públicas [E.C. §§ 48200, 48400 y otros], con consideraciones especiales para los que tienen 16 a 18 años de edad [E.C. § 48410] y se aceptan las alternativas legales que ofrecen las cuatro exenciones que se detallan a continuación.

Cuatro alternativas legales para los educadores en el hogar

1. Los educadores en el hogar pueden establecer una escuela privada con base en su hogar y deberán presentar una declaración jurada de escuela privada ante el Superintendente de Instrucción Pública de California (por lo general el período de presentación es del 1° al 15 de octubre de cada año escolar). Los niños inscriptos en una escuela privada están eximidos de asistir a una escuela pública. De acuerdo con esta disposición [E.C. §§ 48222 y 33190], que se aplica a todas las escuelas privadas:
   a. los instructores deben ser capaces de enseñar;
   b. la instrucción debe brindarse en el idioma inglés (sin embargo consulte más adelante la nota para las familias que no hablan inglés);
   c. la instrucción debe brindarse en las diversas ramas de estudio que se exigen en las escuelas públicas;"
   d. se deben conservar en archivo determinados registros de los estudiantes y de la escuela;

    e. se deben conservar en archivo los formularios del Departamento de Salud (PM 171A y PM 286) [H.S.C. §§ 124085 y 120375].

2. Los padres que opten por la educación en el hogar pueden inscribir a sus hijos/as en un programa satélite de una escuela privada que haya presentado la declaración jurada de escuela privada ante el Superintendente de Instrucción Pública de California [se aplican las mismas exenciones y requisitos legales que en la alternativa (1)]. Estas escuelas satélites se llaman a menudo PSP (programas de satélite de escuelas privadas). Pueden estar totalmente compuestas por educadores en el hogar o ser el programa de extensión de una escuela privada con sede en un campus.

    Técnicamente, ni la alternativa (1) ni la (2) se diferencian en cuanto a una mayor o menor protección o cobertura legal según lo establecido en nuestros Códigos de Educación en vigencia [E.C. §§ 33190 y 48222]. Hay contactos legales y acciones legales recientes que han involucrado a ambos tipos de arreglos. Ambos arreglos son legales pero ambos son constantemente cuestionados. En algunas pocas áreas y casos será más difícil que lo contacten o lo cuestionen legalmente si usted está en un programa tipo PSP. Sin embargo, en base a la experiencia del pasado, es conveniente que todas las familias que educan a sus hijos en el hogar se aseguren la protección de la Asociación de Defensa Legal de la Escuela en el Hogar (por sus siglas en inglés HSLDA). Tanto para la alternativa (1) como para la (2), los padres deberán informar adecuadamente que sus hijos/as están inscriptos en una escuela privada al comunicarse con las escuelas y otros funcionarios públicos.

    A las familias inscriptas en escuelas/programas Fuera del Estado las leyes del Estado de todos modos les exigen estar inscriptos en una escuela privada de California (autónoma con sede en el hogar o satélite/PSP), con una dirección en California para localizarlos. No es necesario ni aconsejable mencionar voluntariamente la inscripción en escuelas/programas fuera del estado. No es ilegal que un residente de California esté inscripto en un programa fuera del estado, siempre que lo haga como una forma de recibir un programa de estudios o determinados servicios y no como un medio de cumplir con la ley.

Los registros de calificaciones del estudiante generados en la escuela pública (llamados archivos cum) pueden enviarse para que los usen los programas fuera del estado, pero nunca son estos programas los que deben enviarlos.

3. Todo padre que eduque a sus hijos/as en el hogar y que posea una credencial válida de maestro en California para todos los grados y material que enseña puede ser exceptuado de acuerdo con la exención de tutoría privada. [E.C. § 48224]

4. El estudiante de educación en el hogar puede inscribirse en un programa de estudio independiente (ISP) de una escuela pública [E.C. §§ 51745-51747] o de una escuela autónoma que ofrezca estudios en el hogar [E.C. § 47600 y otros] si tal opción está disponible en su distrito condado escolar. En estos dos programas, la familia que se educa en el hogar está bajo la total autoridad de las escuelas públicas. Esta opción no nos parece recomendable. Sin embargo, la elección recae en los padres. Hay varios problemas ligados a estos programas de estudios en el hogar de escuelas públicas. Para obtener más detalles, envíe una donación sugerida de $10.00 a los Ministerios de Protección de la Familia (ver la dirección que aparece más abajo) y solicite el paquete informativo "Programas de Estudios Independientes ISP de Escuelas Públicas y Escuelas Autónomas".

Requisitos para las familias que no hablan inglés

Las familias que no hablan inglés pueden preocuparse de no poder cumplir con el requisito de que la instrucción debe brindarse "en el idioma inglés". Sin embargo el E.C. § 30 dispone una excepción:

...toda escuela privada debe determinar cuándo y bajo qué circunstancias la instrucción puede ser de tipo bilingüe.

Es política del Estado asegurarse de que todos los estudiantes adquieran el dominio del idioma inglés en las escuelas, incluyéndose la oferta de una instrucción bilingüe en aquellas situaciones en que tal instrucción resulte educacionalmente ventajosa para los estudiantes. La instrucción bilingüe está autorizada siempre que no interfiera con la instrucción sistemática, secuencial y regular de todos los estudiantes en el idioma inglés.

La regla general para las familias que no hablan inglés es la siguiente: si los padres del niño/a no hablan inglés, la escuela privada puede instruirlo usando la lengua nativa de la familia. Sin embargo, de todos modos deberá brindarse instrucción en inglés, con el objetivo de lograr que el estudiante adquiera destreza en ese idioma. Basándose en este requerimiento, las familias que no hablan inglés pueden aprender juntas como parte de la instrucción regular. En otras palabras, lo adecuado es que la familia use materiales en el idioma que hablan para la mayor parte de las materias y también use un programa para el aprendizaje del inglés como una clase separada hasta lograr el dominio de este idioma.

Problemas legales

Si se consideran la Constitución de Estados Unidos y los estatutos de California, la educación privada con sede en el hogar es legal. Sin embargo, siguen existiendo cuestionamientos que representan una amenaza potencial directa para cualquier educador en California. Estos cuestionamientos se basan en acusaciones **erróneas**, ya sea por ausentismo o por abuso/abandono infantil:

1. Acusación por *Ausentismo habitual* - se lo considera una infracción (cuando no hay antecedentes). [Códigos de Educación de California: E.C. §§ 48260, 48293 y otros]. Esta acusación es aplicada 95% de las veces en los cuestionamientos legales a la educación en el hogar en California.

2. Acusación de violación *del toque de queda diurno* - rara, pero se está haciendo cada vez más común.

3. Acusación de *Abuso/Abandono infantil* - rara, pero puede incluir una pérdida temporal o definitiva de la custodia de los hijos/as.

Recursos

(A) El resto de este manual contiena información detallada sobre las alternativas y requisitos de educación privada legal y el Manual de educación secundaria de CHEA. CHEA tiene un sitio web que puede dar una referencia a una persona que le puede ayudar en español: www.cheaofca.org.

(B) Únase a la *Asociación de defensa legal de la escuela en el hogar (HSLDA)* por sólo $115 cada 12 meses. Hay membresías con descuento. Escriba o llame a HSLDA a: P.O. Box 3000, Purcellville, VA 20134, teléfono: (540) 338-5600.

Únase antes de comenzar su educación en el hogar y antes de retirar a su hijo/a de otra escuela. Es mejor retirarlo durante el verano. Debe unirse a la asociación antes de recibir un cuestionamiento legal a su educación en el hogar, así que hágalo ahora.

En la actualidad HSLDA es la única organización con un plantel de abogados que trabajan a tiempo completo que le asegura una representación inmediata e integral por parte de un abogado con experiencia en esta área del derecho desde el comienzo mismo de cualquier cuestionamiento legal que reciba su educación en el hogar. No hay ningún programa escolar o educativo dentro o fuera del estado disponible para quienes optan por la escolarización privada en California que ofrezca una protección legal absoluta. Aparte del de HSLDA, no hay ningún otro programa/plan de protección legal que garantice la representación de un abogado experto en el tema frente a todos los contactos legales que reciban las familias en relación con su educación en el hogar. HSLDA siempre ha estado en el centro de la defensa de nuestra libertad para optar por la escuela en el hogar en California.

Será la familia individual y no la administración de la escuela satélite/ISP quien será cuestionada por la escuela y otras autoridades. Cada familia debe asumir la responsabilidad de la defensa de su propia familia y asegurar la mejor protección disponible, en particular a la luz del creciente número de derivaciones a los Servicios de Protección Infantil.

(C) La cartilla de *Actualización legal y legislativa* de los Educadores privados y en el hogar de California (en inglés) provee informes de primera mano sobre cualquier cambio en la legislación y sobre las amenazas legales a la educación en el hogar en California. Es una publicación de los Ministerios de Protección de la Familia, la única organización que trabaja en Sacramento a tiempo completo para controlar y ejercer la defensa legal frente a todas las acciones legislativas y administrativas que afectan directamente a los educadores en el hogar de California. Este ministerio cristiano es sostenido en un 100% por donaciones de quienes apoyan la educación privada/en el hogar y los derechos de los padres. Se puede acceder a esta cartilla sin costo comercial mediante una contribución de al menos $40 por año calendario a:

Ministerios de Protección de la Familia
Roy Hanson & Jim Davis
PO Box 730
Lincoln, CA 95648-0730

¿Qué materiales están disponibles?

Los educadores en el hogar pueden valerse de materiales cristianos de calidad, preparados para escuelas cristianas. También se están creando materiales nuevos, o se están adaptando especialmente para uso en el hogar. Los materiales se pueden obtener de tres maneras, básicamente:

Se pueden pedir libros de texto y material didáctico directamente a quienes los publican o a través de compañías de venta por correo. Cada edicion de El Hogar Educador presenta proveedores de materiales educativos.

El hogar educador

En cada amplia edición usted encontrará sugerencias prácticas para la enseñanza, cartas de nuestros lectores que comparten sus pruebas y aliento y ¡mucho más! Para mayor información, pida la revista *El Hogar Educador*, que contiene unos de sus más valiosos recursos para la educación en el hogar.

En México:

APDO 487

2500 Saltillo, Coahuila, Mexico

Teléfono: (844) 483-0377

Fuera de México:

1001 South 10th St., Suite G-529

McAllen, Texas, 78501, USA

Teléfono: 52 (844) 483-0377

Site de Web:

www.ElHogarEducador.org

Un programa de extensión en el hogar ofrecido a través de una escuela cristiana o iglesia local puede proveer material didáctico, servicio de exámenes y asesoría. Si esto no lo ofrece alguna escuela cercana a ti, quizá quieras proponerles la creación de un programa que lo haga.

Materiales, exámenes y asesoría también pueden ser obtenidos a través de cursos cristianos por correspondencia.

Libros de Texto Tradicionales. Pueden conseguirse libros de texto de alta calidad a través de editoriales cristianas. Estos libros tratan a profundidad cada una de las materias en un orden de temas lógico.

Cuadernos de Trabajo. Algunas editoriales han combinado la información del libro de texto con ejercicios escritos en libretas consumibles.

Proveedores de materiales educativos

A Beka Books a/c Publicaciones Aguila

En México:
Sor Juana Inés de la Cruz # 2
Hgo. del Parral, Chihuahua., México.
Teléfono: (627) 522-3150 Fax: (627) 522-4949
ilap@infosel.net.mx

Fuera de México
Casilla de Correo 15068
Asunción, Paraguay
Teléfono: 59 (52) 145-0631
abekaspanish@uninet.com.py

Accelerated Christian Education

P.O. Box 299000-9000
Lewisville, Texas 75029
www.aceministries.com

Christian Light Publications

P.O. Box 1212-MX
Harrisonburg, VA 22801
Teléfono: (540) 343-0768
Fax (540) 433-8896
Office@CLP.org

Colegio Hebrón

9 ave. 29-00, Zona 13 Colonia Santa Fe
Guatemala, Centro América
Teléfono: (502) 333-8392 o 93
colheb@c.net.gt

El Hogar Educador

En México
APDO 17 Arteaga
Coahuila, Mexico, 25350
Teléfono: (844) 483-0377

Fuera de México
1001 South 10th St., Suite G-529
McAllen, Texas 78501 USA
Teléfono: 52 (844) 483-0377
www.ElHogarEducador.org

La Asociación Amós 5:24

Gonzalitos 210-B Norte, Col. Vista Hermosa,
Monterrey, N.L. 64620 México

Librería Nueva Vida

APDO 656 Torreón, Coahuila, México, 27000
Teléfono: (871) 712-7362
robertw@att.net.mx

Lighthouse Christian Academy

P.O. Box 299000-9000
Lewisville, Texas 75029
www.aceministries.com

Literatura Monte Sion

5410 W 11200 N
Tremonton, UT 84337 USA
Teléfono: (435) 257-2185
johnyoder@characterlink.net

Publicadora La Merced

Apartado 15
Pital de San Carlos
Costa Rica, C.A.
Teléfono: (506) 465-0017; Fax: (506) 465-0018
plmantor@racsa.co.cr.

Publicadores Lámpara y Luz

26 RD 5577
Farmington, NM 87401
Teléfono: (505) 632-3521 Fax: (505) 632-1246
lamplight@cyberport.com

Respuestas en Génesis

www.RespuestasEnGenesis.org

Vara y Cayado

Hwy 172
Crockett, Kentucky 41413 USA
Teléfono: (606) 522-4348 Fax (606) 522-4896

Mike & Pam Richardson, Vida Nueva Ministries

1001 S 10th Street, Suite G-529
McAllen, Texas 78501

Appendix C

Samples and Blank Forms

All of the forms in this book are available online
at the CHEA website, www.cheaofca.org/forms

Samples and Forms for School Records

While some school records are required, you can keep them in whatever format works well for you. The samples included here are just for ideas. Feel free to make copies of any blank forms for your own family's personal use, or design your own.

Also note that there are several different samples for many of the records. You certainly don't need all of these. Some homeschoolers like one style, others like a different style. If you're just starting out, choose one that looks easy to you and that does the job. You can always adjust your forms for next year if you find that you'd like something a little different.

Downloadable PDF files of these forms can be found at www.cheaofca.org/forms.

Course of Study - Grades 1-6

Bible	• Learn basic biblical doctrines, including salvation • Learn the books of the Bible • Memorize important Scripture verses • Participate in regular fellowship • Learn Christian character and demonstrate spiritual growth
English	• Learn how to read, write, and communicate orally • Read independently from a variety of kinds of materials • Understand the importance and uses of written communication • Learn to speak in individual, small group, and public settings • Learn the basic skills of spelling, grammar, and penmanship • Begin a foundation of good composition skills
Arithmetic	• Master the basic arithmetic operations of counting, addition, subtraction, multiplication, and division • Learn the practical uses of arithmetic such as time, money, measurements, etc.
Social Science	• Study basic local, state, U.S., and world history • Study the concept of community and our place in it • Learn basic geography skills • Study basics of government and economics
Science	• Study the basic concepts of science, including research and experimentation, across the disciplines of biology, chemistry, and physics, using hands-on activities • Develop an appreciation for God's creation
Fine Arts	• Introduce various art media such as drawing, painting, sculpting, dancing, music, and more • Teach appreciation for beauty
Health	• Learn basics of hygiene and nutrition • Learn basic body parts
Physical Education	• Learn the value of regular exercise and develop a habit of physical fitness

An Introduction to Home Education, 12th Edition Revised, 2014

Course of Study - Grades 1-6

Bible	
English	
Arithmetic	
Social Science	
Science	
Fine Arts	
Health	
Physical Education	

Course of Study - Grades 7-12

Bible	•Learn basic biblical doctrines, including salvation •Memorize Scripture verses •Participate in regular fellowship •Learn Christian character and demonstrate spiritual growth •Develop a biblical worldview and apply it consistently
English	•Master skills of reading, writing, and oral communication •Master spelling, grammar, and penmanship •Study American and world literature
Arithmetic	•Master the basic arithmetic operations and practical uses of arithmetic. •Study advanced mathematics such as algebra and geometry
Social Science	•Learn the fundamentals of U.S. and world history •Master basic geography skills •Study government and economics
Science	•Study the basic disciplines of biology, chemistry, and physics •Develop an appreciation for God's creation
Fine Arts	•Introduce various art media such as drawing, painting, sculpting, dancing, music, and more •Teach appreciation for beauty
Health	•Learn basics of hygiene and nutrition •Learn basic anatomy
Physical Education	•Learn the value of regular exercise and develop a habit of physical fitness
Foreign Language	•Study a foreign language and the culture of the country or setting in which it is spoken
Applied Arts	•Introduce several applied arts, such as carpentry, computer graphics, sewing, and others •Master those basic applied arts that are used by all adults
Career/ Technical	•Learn basic computer and typing skills •Work to earn money and handle a budget
Parenting Skills	•Learn family living skills such as child and elder care, •Learn home economics skills for running a home

An Introduction to Home Education, 12th Edition Revised, 2014

Course of Study - Grades 7-12

Bible	
English	
Arithmetic	
Social Science	
Science	
Fine Arts	
Health	
Physical Education	
Foreign Language	
Applied Arts	
Career/ Technical	
Parenting Skills	

Elementary Proposed Course of Study

Student: Joseph Homeschooler

School Year: 2012-2013   **Grade:** 6

Subject	Book Title	Publisher	Level	Semester	
Bible Application Memory	Those Courageous Christians A Study of Acts	by William Coleman		X	X
English Reading, Spelling, Literature, Penmanship, Composition	English for Christian Schools Reading for Christian Schools	Bob Jones University Press	6 6	X X	X X
Arithmetic Calculations, Problem Solving	Math 6/5	Hake-Saxon	5-6	X	X
Social Science History Geography	See reading list for biographies, historical fiction, and history books read	multiple		X	X
Science Life Science	God's Marvelous Works	Rod & Staff	5		X
Fine Arts Appreciation Art Music	Music of the Masters Piano Lessons			X X	X
Health Nutrition Personal Hygiene Safety	Informally				
Physical Education Motor Skills Sports Knowledge	City Soccer Sports Days Little League Baseball			X	X

Comments:
Joe will be focusing more on writing skills this year. (composition, grammar)

An Introduction to Home Education, 12th Edition Revised, 2014

Elementary Proposed Course of Study

Student: _____

School Year: _____ **Grade:** _____

Subject	Book Title	Publisher	Level	Semester	
Bible					
English					
Arithmetic					
Social Science					
Science					
Fine Arts					
Health					
Physical Education					
Comments:					

Jr/Sr High Proposed Course of Study

Student: Jane Homeschooler

School Year: 2009-2010   **Grade:** 11

Subject	Book Title	Publisher	Semester	
Bible Application Memory	LifePac Bible Doctrine	Alpha Omega	X	X
English World Literature, Composition	Backgrounds to World Literature	ABeka	X	X
Math Algebra	Principles from Patterns: Algebra	Cornerstone Curriculum	X	X
Social Science World History and Geography	World History for Christian Schools	Bob Jones University Press	X	X
Science Biology	Biology	Apologia	X	X
Elective Foreign Language: French	Nouveaux Chemins	ABeka	X	X
Elective				
Physical Education	Workouts at Gym	Family Fitness Center	X	X
Comments:				

An Introduction to Home Education, 12th Edition Revised, 2014

Jr/Sr High Proposed Course of Study

Student: _____

School Year: _____ **Grade:** _____

Subject	Book Title	Publisher	Semester	
Bible				
English				
Math				
Social Science				
Science				
Elective				
Elective				
Physical Education				
Comments:				

Proposed School Year Calendar

Last Name: _Homeschooler_

Children's Names: _Jane, Joseph, John, and Jimmy_

School Year: _2009-2010_

Proposed number of school days: _177_

Instructions:

Write in weekends, holidays, and vacations for the school year on the calendar below. Then highlight the days you plan to have school. Write the totals at the end of each row.

Days/Months	1	2	3	4	5	6	7	8	9	10	11	12	13	14	15	16	17	18	19	20	21	22	23	24	25	26	27	28	29	30	31	Total this month	Total to Date
August	W	W	-	-	-	-	-	W	W	-	-	-	-	-	W	W						W	W						W	W		11	11
September			W	W	W	W						W	W						W	W						W	W					22	33
October			W	W	W	W	W	W		W	W	W	W		W		W	W	W		W	W		W	W	W	W				W	22	55
November	W						W	W				W	W	W	W	W	W	H	W	W	W	W	W	W	H	H	H	W	W			18	73
December			W						W	W		W	W	H	H	H	H	H	W	W	H	H	H	H	H	H	W	H	H	H	H	9	82
January	H	W	W													W				W	W	W	W	W	W	>	W	W	W	W	W	20	102
February						W	W	W			W		W	W				W	W	W	W	>	>	>	>	W	W	W				15	117
March				W		W	W			W	W		W	W		W	W	W	W	W	W						W	W		W		23	140
April			W	W	W						W				W	W	W	W	W			W	W	W	W	W	W		W	W		17	157
May	W	W	W	W	W	W	-	-	-	-	-	W	W	-	W	-	W	-	W	-	-	W	W	W	W	W	W	-	W	W	-	20	177
June	-	-	W	-	W	-	-	-	-	-	W	-	-	W	-	-	-	W	W	-	-	-	-	-	-	-	-	-	-	-			
July	-	-	W	W	-	-	-	-	-	W	W	-	-	W	-	-	W	W	-	-	-	-	-	-	W	-	-	-	-	-	W		

Proposed School Year Calendar

Last Name: _____

School Year: _____

Children's Names: _____
_____
_____

Proposed number of school days: _____

Instructions:

Write in weekends and holidays for the school year on the calendar below. Then highlight the days you plan to have school. Write the totals at the end of each row.

Days/ Months	1	2	3	4	5	6	7	8	9	10	11	12	13	14	15	16	17	18	19	20	21	22	23	24	25	26	27	28	29	30	31	Total this month	Total to Date
August																																	
September																																	
October																																	
November																																	
December																																	
January																																	
February																																	
March																																	
April																																	
May																																	
June																																	
July																																	

Proposed School Year Calendar

School Name: Harborview Christian School

School Year: 2012-2013   **Proposed Days:** 160

Write in the months and dates on the calendar below. Then highlight the days you plan to have school. Write the totals at the bottom of each month.

August

S	M	Tu	W	TH	F	S
						1
2	3	4	5	6	7	8
9	10	11	12	13	14	15
16	17	18	19	20	21	22
23	24	25	26	27	28	29
30	31					

This month: 0   To date: 0

September

S	M	Tu	W	TH	F	S
		1	2	3	4	5
6	7	8	9	10	11	12
13	14	15	16	17	18	19
20	21	22	23	24	25	26
27	28	29	30			

This month: 18   To date: 18

October

S	M	Tu	W	TH	F	S
				1	2	3
4	5	6	7	8	9	10
11	12	13	14	15	16	17
18	19	20	21	22	23	24
25	26	27	28	29	30	31

This month: 17   To date: 35

November

S	M	Tu	W	TH	F	S
1	2	3	4	5	6	7
8	9	10	11	12	13	14
15	16	17	18	19	20	21
22	23	24	25	26	27	28
29	30					

This month: 16   To date: 51

December

S	M	Tu	W	TH	F	S
		1	2	3	4	5
6	7	8	9	10	11	12
13	14	15	16	17	18	19
20	21	22	23	24	25	26
27	28	29	30	31		

This month: 14   To date: 65

January

S	M	Tu	W	TH	F	S
					1	2
3	4	5	6	7	8	9
10	11	12	13	14	15	16
17	18	19	20	21	22	23
24	25	26	27	28	29	30
31						

This month: 20   To date: 85

February

S	M	Tu	W	TH	F	S
	1	2	3	4	5	6
7	8	9	10	11	12	13
14	15	16	17	18	19	20
21	22	23	24	25	26	27
28						

This month: 15   To date: 95

March

S	M	Tu	W	TH	F	S
	1	2	3	4	5	6
7	8	9	10	11	12	13
14	15	16	17	18	19	20
21	22	23	24	25	26	27
28	29	30	31			

This month: 23   To date: 118

April

S	M	Tu	W	TH	F	S
				1	2	3
4	5	6	7	8	9	10
11	12	13	14	15	16	17
18	19	20	21	22	23	24
25	26	27	28	29	30	

This month: 17   To date: 135

May

S	M	Tu	W	TH	F	S
						1
2	3	4	5	6	7	8
9	10	11	12	13	14	15
16	17	18	19	20	21	22
23	24	25	26	27	28	29
30	31					

This month: 20   To date: 155

June

S	M	Tu	W	TH	F	S
		1	2	3	4	5
6	7	8	9	10	11	12
13	14	15	16	17	18	19
20	21	22	23	24	25	26
27	28	29	30			

This month: 9   To date: 164

July

S	M	Tu	W	TH	F	S
				1	2	3
4	5	6	7	8	9	10
11	12	13	14	15	16	17
18	19	20	21	22	23	24
25	26	27	28	29	30	31

This month: To date:

An Introduction to Home Education, 12th Edition Revised, 2014

Proposed School Year Calendar

School Name: _____

School Year: _____   **Proposed Days:** _____

Write in weekends and holidays for the school year on the calendar below. Then highlight the days you plan to have school. Write the totals at the end of each row.

S	M	Tu	W	TH	F	S

This month: _____   To date: _____

S	M	Tu	W	TH	F	S

This month: _____   To date: _____

S	M	Tu	W	TH	F	S

This month: _____   To date: _____

S	M	Tu	W	TH	F	S

This month: _____   To date: _____

S	M	Tu	W	TH	F	S

This month: _____   To date: _____

S	M	Tu	W	TH	F	S

This month: _____   To date: _____

S	M	Tu	W	TH	F	S

This month: _____   To date: _____

S	M	Tu	W	TH	F	S

This month: _____   To date: _____

S	M	Tu	W	TH	F	S

This month: _____   To date: _____

S	M	Tu	W	TH	F	S

This month: _____   To date: _____

S	M	Tu	W	TH	F	S

This month: _____   To date: _____

S	M	Tu	W	TH	F	S

This month: _____   To date: _____

Attendance Record

Last Name: Homeschooler

School Year: 2009-2010

Children's Names: Jane, Joseph, John, and Jimmy

X = Present   A = School Day Absence

Days/Months	1	2	3	4	5	6	7	8	9	10	11	12	13	14	15	16	17	18	19	20	21	22	23	24	25	26	27	28	29	30	31	Total this month	Total to Date
August		X	X	X													X	X	X	X	X			X	X	X	X	X			X	11	11
September		X	X	X				X	X	X	X			X	X	X	X	X	X		A	A	X	X	X	X			X	X		20	31
October	X	X		X		X	X	X	X	X		X	X	X	X	X	X	X	X	X	X	X	X	X		X	X	X	X	X	X	22	53
November		X	X	X		X			X	X	X	X	X	X	X	X	X	X	X	X			X	X						X		18	71
December	X	X	X	X			X	X	X	X	X																					9	80
January						X	X	X	X	X	X	X	X	X	X		X	X	X	A	A	A	X	X	X	X	X	X	X			17	97
February	X	X	X	X				X	X	X	X	X	X	X	X	X	X	X	X		X											15	112
March	X	X	X	X			X	X	X	X	X	X	X	X	X	X	X	X	X	X	X	X	X	X	X	X			X	X	X	23	135
April	X	X	X			X	X	X	X	X		X	X	X			X	X	X	X	X	X	X	X	X	X	X	X	X	X		22	157
May			X	X		X	X			X							X	X			X		X	X	X	X	X	X				20	177
June																																	
July																																	

Attendance Record

Last Name: _____

School Year: _____

X = Present   A = School Day Absence

Days/Months	1	2	3	4	5	6	7	8	9	10	11	12	13	14	15	16	17	18	19	20	21	22	23	24	25	26	27	28	29	30	31	Total this month	Total to Date
August																																	
September																																	
October																																	
November																																	
December																																	
January																																	
February																																	
March																																	
April																																	
May																																	
June																																	
July																																	

Children's Names: _____

Samples and Forms for Teaching Records

None of the records depicted in this section's samples are legally required ones. But as was discussed in chapter three, you'll need some way to keep track of what you want to do each week and what you've completed. We could include hundreds of samples of teaching records; it seems every teacher has their own way of doing it. You don't even need a fancy form at all — a lined piece of paper will do the job. But it *is* nice to have something that looks organized even if the way you teach is very informal. Good records seem to give confidence by making you feel prepared to teach.

Most of the forms in this section can easily be adapted to be either a plan that you fill out in advance and as a check-off sheet after assignments are completed, or as a journal which you fill out after each day's lessons have been completed.

As with the school records section, choose what looks easy to use and go with that. You can always change things around as you go.

You are welcome to make copies of sheets in this section for your own family's use.

Lesson Plan Diary

Name: John Homeschooler   **Beginning Date:** 10/5/13   **Week:** 9

Day	Subject	Assignment
Monday	Bible	Read Luke 12 Read Ch 1: "Basic Christianity" Verse: Luke 12:31
	English	Read pp 108-109 Practices 1-3, pp 110-112 Exercise 69
	Math	Read pp 16-17 Exercise 12
	Science	Read pp 12-17 Experiment on p 17
	Foods	Study "Cooking Tools" in front of cookbook. Plan dinner for Fri.
	P.E.	Running
Tuesday	Bible	Read Luke 13 Discuss "Basic Christianity" Prayer journal
	English	Read page 114 Practices 1-2, p 115 Exercise 70
	Math	Read pp 20-21 Exercise 13
	History	Read pp 45-56 Complete map of Europe at beginning of WWII
	Foods	Make shopping list for Thurs. Check budget
	P.E.	Wt. Training class at gym
Wednesday	Bible	Read Luke 14 Recite memory verse Bible study tonight
	English	Read page 115-117 Practices 3-5, p 117 Exercise 71
	Math	Read pp 24-25 Exercise 14
	Science	Read pp 18-24
	Foods	Shop for menu items Fill in budget
	P.E.	Running
Thursday	Bible	Read Luke 15 Read Ch 2: "Basic Christianity"
	English	Read page 120-124 Practices 1-2, p 121 Exercise 72
	Math	Read pp 28-29 Exercise 15
	History	Read pp 57-70 Watch video on WWII
	Foods	Your turn to cook!
	P.E.	Soccer practice
Friday	Bible	Read Luke 16 Discuss "Basic Christianity" Recite verse
	English	Write essay on Shakespeare
	Math	Read pp 32-33 Chapter Quiz
	Science	Read pp 25-30 Prepare for test on Monday
	Foods	Write-up of last night's meal
	P.E.	Running
Notes	Piano practice on Monday-Thursday, Lesson on Friday	
	Soccer game on Saturday morning	

An Introduction to Home Education, 12th Edition Revised, 2014

Lesson Plan Diary

Name: _____ Beginning Date: _____ Week: _____

Day	Subject	Assignment
Monday		
Tuesday		
Wednesday		
Thursday		
Friday		
Notes		

Lesson Plan by Subject

Name: Jimmy Homeschooler   **Subject:** History

Read	Do	Date	Done
UHW6.	Study and memorize Nicene and Apostles' Creeds	10/4	X
pp. 301-304			
WHCS			
pp. 114-118	Answer questions 3-6, p. 119	10/5	X
UHW6	(The New Testament)	10/5	X
pp. 305-307			
MARR, Card 1	(Conversion of St. Augustine)	10/6	X
UHW6	(Great Church Fathers)	10/6	X
pp. 308-312			
MARR, Ch. 01,	(Project 1)	10/7	X
pp. 3-4	Discuss #1-3 after reading assignment	10/7	X
CIH, pp. 35-39	Answer question 7, p. 42	10/7	X
MARR, Ch. 01			
pp. 9-10	Test, answer all questions in complete sentences.	10/8	X
Notes:	MARR = Middle Ages, Renaissance and Reformation WHCS = World History for Christian Schools (BJUP) UHW6 = Universal History of the World, Vol. 6 CIH = The Church in History		

Lesson Plan by Subject

Name: _____   Subject: _____

Read	Do	Date	Done

Notes:

Weekly Lesson Plan

Name: John Homeschooler   Beginning Date: 10/5/09   Week: 9

Subj	Monday	Tuesday	Wednesday	Thursday	Friday	Notes
Bible	Read Luke 12 Read Ch 1: "Basic Christianity" Verse: Luke 12:31	Read Luke 13 Discuss "Basic Christianity" Prayer journal	Read Luke 14 Recite memory verse Bible study tonight	Read Luke 15 Read Ch 2: "Basic Christianity"	Read Luke 16 Discuss "Basic Christianity" Recite verse	Piano practice on Monday-Thursday, Lesson on Friday

Soccer game on Saturday morning |
Eng	Read pp 108-109 Practices 1-3, pp 110-112 Exercise 69	Read page 114 Practices 1-2, p 115 Exercise 70	Read page 115-117 Practices 3-5, p 117 Exercise 71	Read page 120-124 Practices 1-2, p 121 Exercise 72	Write essay on Shakespeare	
Math	Read pp 16-17 Exercise 12	Read pp 20-21 Exercise 13	Read pp 24-25 Exercise 14	Read pp 28-29 Exercise 15	Read pp 32-33 Chapter Quiz	
Sci	Read pp 12-17 Experiment on p 17		Read pp 18-24		Read pp 25-30 Prepare for test on Monday	
Hist		Read pp 45-56 Complete map of Europe at beginning of WWII		Read pp 57-70 Watch video on WWII		
Foods	Study "Cooking Tools" in front of cookbook. Plan dinner for Fri.	Make shopping list for Thurs. Check budget	Shop for menu items Fill in budget	Your turn to cook!	Write-up of last night's meal	
P.E.	Running	Wt. Training class at gym	Running	Soccer practice	Running	

An Introduction to Home Education, 12th Edition Revised, 2014

Weekly Lesson Plan

Name: _____

Beginning Date: _____

Week: _____

Subj	Monday	Tuesday	Wednesday	Thursday	Friday	Notes

Weekly Lesson Plan

Name: John Homeschooler

Subject & Source	Monday	Tuesday
Bible		
Bible Reading	Read Luke 12	Read Luke 13
Basic Christianity	Read Ch 1"	Discuss Ch 1
Memory Verse	Luke 12:31	Prayer journal
Eng		
BJU Text	Read pp 108-109 Practices 1-3, pp 110-112	Read page 114 Practices 1-2, p 115
Grammar Workbook	Exercise 69	Exercise 70
Math		
Algebra II Text	Read pp 16-17 Exercise 12	Read pp 20-21 Exercise 13
Sci		
Apologia Biology	Read pp 12-17 Experiment on p 17	
Hist		
A Beka World Hist.		Read pp 45-56 Complete map of Europe at beginning of WWII
Home Ec		
Joy of Cooking	Study "Cooking Tools" in front of cookbook. Plan dinner for Thurs.	Make shopping list for Thurs.
Home Budget		Check budget
P.E.		
Family Fitness Gym		Weight Training class
	Running	

Beginning Date: _10/5/13_   **Week:** _9_

Wednesday	Thursday	Friday
Read Luke 14 Recite memory verse	Read Luke 15 Read Ch 2	Read Luke 16 Discuss Ch 2 Recite verse
Read page 115-117 Practices 3-5, p 117 Exercise 71	Read page 120-124 Practices 1-2, p 121 Exercise 72	Write essay on Shakespeare
Read pp 24-25 Exercise 14	Read pp 28-29 Exercise 15	Read pp 32-33 Chapter Quiz
Read pp 18-24		Read pp 25-30 Prepare for test on Monday
	Read pp 57-70 Watch video on WWII	
Shop for menu items Fill in budget	Your turn to cook!	Write-up of last night's meal
Running	Soccer practice	Running

Weekly Lesson Plan

Name: _____

Subject & Source	Monday	Tuesday

An Introduction to Home Education, 12th Edition Revised, 2014

Beginning Date: _____ **Week:** _____

Wednesday	Thursday	Friday

Daily Diary

Name John Homeschooler

Date	Activity
11/16/2013	Read Little Visits with God (LVWG), pp. 39-41 (Discussed God's love and meaning of word "love")
	Read The Tale of the Faithful Dove, by Beatrix Potter
	Read Christopher Columbus by Ceserani
	Drew pictures of Columbus' ships using ruler and measuring concepts.
11/19	Read LVWG pp. 42-43 (Discussed meaning of words: wrath, anger, clamor and evil speaking.)
	Read Adventures with a Straw, by Harry Milgrum
	Did experiments with straws
11/26	Played Alphabet Bingo
	Played math game using concepts in addition, subtraction, multiplication and division
11/27	Library Day
11/28	Field Trip to Fire Station (Careers in Neighborhood)
	Read Great Names in American History (Capt. John Smith & Miles Standish)
	Read Black Beauty, Ch. 5
	Bible Reading
11/29	Bible Reading
	Made Pilgrim Collars & Hats
	Shopped for Pilgrim food (learned price comparison).
11/30	Made Pilgrim's Corn Pudding & Cranberry Sauce (learned number and fraction concepts while measuring).
	Discussed meaning of seasons, particularly fall, as we walked in the park (studied leaves, etc.).
	Experiment in making rain.
	Listened to a Beethoven concerto while completing chores.
12/3	Thanksgiving - School Holiday
12/4	Holiday

Daily Diary

Name_____

Date	Activity

Reading Record

Name_____

Date Completed	Title	Author & Publisher

Extra-Curricular Activities Record

Name_____

Date	Subject	Grade/Age	Activity

Field Trip Record

Name_____ **Grade** _____ **School Year** _____

Date	Location	Activity

An Introduction to Home Education, 12th Edition Revised, 2014

Samples and Forms for Pupil Records

The samples in this section show only a couple of ways to keep records and there are actually many ways. Use what you like or make your own.

You are welcome to make copies of sheets in this section for your own family's use.

Elementary Cumulative Record

School: Harborview Christian School   1234 Elm Street, Anaheim, CA 92803

Student: Homeschooler, Joseph Lee

Birthdate: 09/21/2000

Address: 1234 Elm Street, Anaheim, CA 92803

Place of Birth: Anaheim, CA

Parents: Jack and Jill Homeschooler

Gender: X Male   ___ Female

School Year 2006-07 | Grade: 1 | Start Date: 8/1/6 | End Date: 6/8/7 | Attendance: 177

Subject	Sem 1	Sem 2
Bible	B	B
Language Arts/ Reading	B	B
Arithmetic	C	C
Social Studies	C	B
Science	A	A
P.E.	A	A

School Year 2007-08 | Grade: 2 | Start Date: 8/2/7 | End Date: 5/19/8 | Attendance: 162

Subject	Sem 1	Sem 2
Bible	A	B
Language Arts/ Reading	B	B
Arithmetic	B	B
Social Studies	C	C
Science	B	A
P.E.	A	A

School Year 2008-09 | Grade: 3 | Start Date: 9/4/8 | End Date: 6/2/9 | Attendance: 174

Subject	Sem 1	Sem 2
Bible	B	B
Language Arts/ Reading	B	B
Arithmetic	C	C
Social Studies	B	C
Science	A	B
P.E.	A	A

School Year _____ | Grade: ____ | Start Date: ____ | End Date: ____ | Attendance: ____

Subject	Sem 1	Sem 2

School Year _____ | Grade: ____ | Start Date: ____ | End Date: ____ | Attendance: ____

Subject	Sem 1	Sem 2

An Introduction to Home Education, 12th Edition Revised, 2014

Elementary Cumulative Record

School: _____

Student: _____

Address: _____

Parents: _____

Birthdate: _____

Place of Birth: _____

Gender: _____ Male _____ Female

School Year		Grade:		
Start Date:	End Date:		Attendance:	
Subject			Sem 1	Sem 2

School Year		Grade:		
Start Date:	End Date:		Attendance:	
Subject			Sem 1	Sem 2

School Year		Grade:		
Start Date:	End Date:		Attendance:	
Subject			Sem 1	Sem 2

School Year		Grade:		
Start Date:	End Date:		Attendance:	
Subject			Sem 1	Sem 2

Middle School Cumulative Record

School: ___Harborview Christian School, 1234 Elm Street, Anaheim, CA 92803___

Student: ___Homeschooler, Jane Anne___

Address: ___1234 Elm Street, Anaheim, CA 92803___

Birthdate: ___11/14/1996___   Place of Birth: ___Anaheim, CA___

Parents: ___Jack and Jill Homeschooler___   Gender: ___ Male   _X_ Female

School Year **2006-07**		Grade: **6**	Attendance: **177**	
Start Date: **8/16/06**		End Date: **6/8/07**		
Semester 1		**Semester 2**		
Subject	Grade	Subject		Grade
Bible	A	Bible		A
English 6a	B	English 6b		B
Arithmetic 6a	B	Arithmetic 6b		C
World History	C	Life Science		C
Sewing	B	Quilting		B
Piano - Int.	A	Piano - Int.		A
P.E.	B	P.E.		B

School Year **2007-08**		Grade: **7**	Attendance: **162**	
Start Date: **8/2/07**		End Date: **5/19/07**		
Semester 1		**Semester 2**		
Subject	Grade	Subject		Grade
Bible	A	Bible		B
English 7a	B	English 7b		A
Arithmetic 7a	B	Arithmetic 7b		B
Geography	C	Astronomy		C
Cooking 1	B	Cooking 2		B
Piano - Adv.	A	Piano - Adv.		B
P.E.	B	P.E.		B

School Year **2008-09**		Grade: **8**	Attendance: **174**	
Start Date: **9/4/08**		End Date: **6/2/09**		
Semester 1		**Semester 2**		
Subject	Grade	Subject		Grade
Bible	A	Bible		A
English 8a	B	English 8b		B
Arithmetic 8a	B	Arithmetic 8b		C
California History and Government	C	Horticulture		A
Advanced Cooking 1	B	Advanced Cooking 2		A
Piano - Adv.	A	Piano - Adv.		A
P.E.	B	P.E.		B

An Introduction to Home Education, 12th Edition Revised, 2014

Middle School Cumulative Record

School: _____

Student: _____

Address: _____

Birthdate: _____ **Place of Birth:** _____

Parents: _____ **Gender:** ___ Male ___ Female

School Year		Grade:		Attendance:
Start Date:		End Date:		
Semester 1		**Semester 2**		
Subject	Grade	**Subject**	Grade	

School Year		Grade:		Attendance:
Start Date:		End Date:		
Semester 1		**Semester 2**		
Subject	Grade	**Subject**	Grade	

School Year		Grade:		Attendance:
Start Date:		End Date:		
Semester 1		**Semester 2**		
Subject	Grade	**Subject**	Grade	

High School Transcript

School: Harborview Christian School
Student: Joan Marie Homeschooler
Address: 1234 Elm St., Anaheim, CA 92803
Birthdate May 13, 1991 **Gender:** Female

Grade: 9 School Year 2005/2006 Start Date: 09/14/2005 End Date: 05/22/2006

Semester 1			Semester 2		
Subject	Grade	Credits	Subject	Grade	Credits
Bible: OT Survey 1	A	5	Bible: OT Survey 2	B	5
English 9a	B	5	English 9b	B	5
World History 1	B	5	World History 2	B	5
Physical Science	B	5	Horticulture	B	5
Algebra 1a	A	5	Algebra 1b	C	5
German 1a	B	5	German 1b	B	5
P.E.	B	5	P.E.	A	5
Sem 1 Credits: 35			Sem 2 Credits: 35		
Cum Credits: 35			Cum Credits: 70		
Sem 1 GPA: 3.33			Sem 2 GPA: 2.83		
Cum GPA: 3.33			Cum GPA: 3.08		

Grade: 10 School Year 2006/2007 Start Date: 08/12/2006 End Date: 05/23/2007

Semester 1			Semester 2		
Subject	Grade	Credits	Subject	Grade	Credits
Bible: NT Survey 1	A	5	Bible: NT Survey 2	A	5
English 10a	B	5	English 10b	B	5
U.S. History 1	C	5	U.S. History 2	B	5
Biology 1	B	5	Biology 2	B	5
Algebra 2a	C	5	Algebra 2b	C	5
German 2a	B	5	German 2b	B	5
P.E.	B	5	P.E.	A	5
Sem 1 GPA: 2.83			Sem 2 GPA: 3.0		
Cum GPA: 3.0			Cum GPA: 3.0		
Sem 1 Credits: 35			Sem 2 Credits: 35		
Cum Credits: 105			Cum Credits: 140		

Grade: 11 School Year 2007/2008 Start Date: 09/02/2007 End Date: 06/10/2008

Semester 1			Semester 2		
Subject	Grade	Credits	Subject	Grade	Credits
Bible: Worldview 1	B	5	Bible: Worldview 2	A	5
English 11a	B	5	English 11b	B	5
Chemistry 1	C	5	Chemistry 2	C	5
Geometry 1	C	5	Geometry 2	B	5
Home Economics 1	A	5	Home Economics 2	A	5
Beginning Guitar	B	5	P.E.	A	5
P.E.	B	5			
Sem 1 GPA: 2.83			Sem 2 GPA: 3.2		
Cum GPA: 2.96			Cum GPA: 3.0		
Sem 1 Credits: 35			Sem 2 Credits: 30		
Cum Credits: 175			Cum Credits: 205		

Grade: 12 School Year 2008/2009 Start Date: 08/22/2008 End Date: 05/25/2009

Semester 1			Semester 2		
Subject	Grade	Credits	Subject	Grade	Credits
Bible: Christian Living 1	A	5	Bible: Christian Living 2	B	5
American Literature 1	B	5	American Literature 2	B	5
Practical Math Skills 1a	A	5	Practical Math Skills 1b	A	5
Physics 1a	B	5	Physics 1b	C	5
Driver Education	A	5	Work Experience	A	5
Health	A	5	P.E.	A	5
P.E.	B	5			
Sem 1 GPA: 3.67			Sem 2 GPA: 3.2		
Cum GPA: 3.10			Cum GPA: 3.11		
Sem 1 Credits: 35			Sem 2 Credits: 30		
Cum Credits: 240			Cum Credits: 270		

An Introduction to Home Education, 12th Edition Revised, 2014

High School Transcript

School: _____

Address: _____

Student: _____

Birthdate _____

Gender: _____

Block 1

Grade: _____ School Year _____ Start Date: _____ End Date: _____

Semester 1				Semester 2		
Subject	Grade	Credits		Subject	Grade	Credits
Sem 1 Credits:				Sem 2 Credits:		
Cum Credits:				Cum Credits:		
Sem 1 GPA:				Sem 2 GPA:		
Cum GPA:				Cum GPA:		

Block 2

Grade: _____ School Year _____ Start Date: _____ End Date: _____

Semester 1				Semester 2		
Subject	Grade	Credits		Subject	Grade	Credits
Sem 1 Credits:				Sem 2 Credits:		
Cum Credits:				Cum Credits:		
Sem 1 GPA:				Sem 2 GPA:		
Cum GPA:				Cum GPA:		

Block 3

Grade: _____ School Year _____ Start Date: _____ End Date: _____

Semester 1				Semester 2		
Subject	Grade	Credits		Subject	Grade	Credits
Sem 1 Credits:				Sem 2 Credits:		
Cum Credits:				Cum Credits:		
Sem 1 GPA:				Sem 2 GPA:		
Cum GPA:				Cum GPA:		

Block 4

Grade: _____ School Year _____ Start Date: _____ End Date: _____

Semester 1				Semester 2		
Subject	Grade	Credits		Subject	Grade	Credits
Sem 1 Credits:				Sem 2 Credits:		
Cum Credits:				Cum Credits:		
Sem 1 GPA:				Sem 2 GPA:		
Cum GPA:				Cum GPA:		

High School Transcript

School: Harborview Christian School
Address: 1234 Elm St., Anaheim, CA 92803

Student: Joan Marie Homeschooler
Birthdate May 13, 1991 **Gender: Female**

Subject Area	Req	Course Title	Grade	Credits
Bible	40	OT Survey	B+	10
		NT Survey	A	10
		Worldview	B	10
		Christian Living	A	10
English	40	English 1	B	10
		English 2	B	10
		English 3	B	10
		American Literature	B	10
Math	20	Algebra 1	B	10
		Algebra 2	C	10
		Geometry	B-	10
Social Studies	20	World History	B	10
		U.S. History	B-	10
Science	20	Physical Science	B	5
		Horticulture	B	5
		Biology	B	10
		Chemistry	C	10
		Physics	C+	10
Foreign Language	10	German 1	B	10
		German 2	B	10

Subject Area	Req	Course Title	Grade	Credits
Physical Education	40	P.E. 9	B+	10
		P.E. 10	A-	10
		P.E. 11	B	10
		P.E. 12	A	10
Electives	40	Home Economics	A	10
		Beginning Guitar	B	5
		Health	A	5
		Driver Education	A	5
		Work Experience	A	5
		Also see Math, Science, & Foreign Language		

Credits Required: 230	Total Credits Earned: 230
Grad. Requirements Met: 05/25/2009	GPA: 3.55
Diploma Awarded:	High School Diploma: 06/10/2009
Exams:	CHSPE: 05/15/2008 -- passed
	SAT: 11/15/2008 -- V650 M680
Extra Curricular:	
Church youth group leader, Bible Study Fellowship, Debate Team	

An Introduction to Home Education, 12th Edition Revised, 2014

High School Transcript

School: _____

Address: _____

Student: _____

Birthdate: _____

Gender: _____

Subject Area	Req	Course Title	Grade	Credits

Subject Area	Req	Course Title	Grade	Credits

Credits Required:	Total Credits Earned:
Grad. Requirements Met:	GPA:
Diploma Awarded:	
Exams:	
Extra Curricular:	

High School Transcript

School: **Harborview Christian School**
1234 Elm St., Anaheim, CA 92803

Student: **Jennifer Ann Homeschooler**
Date of Birth: 05/13/1991   Gender: Female

High School Courses Taken Prior to Grade 9:

GPA: 3.80   Credits: 25

Subject	Grade	Credits
English: Journalism	B	5
Algebra 1-2	A	10
Intro to Computers & Programming	A	10

Grade: 9   School Year: 2005/2006   Start Date: 09/14/2005   End Date: 05/22/2006

SEMESTER 1

Subject	Grade	Credits
Bible: The Pentateuch	A	5
English: Comp & Grammer 9a	B	5
Geography 1	B	5
Astronomy	B	5
Algebra 3	A	5
Latin 1	B	5
P.E.	C	5

Sem. 1 GPA: 3.33   Sem. 1 Credits: 35
Cum GPA: 3.55   Cum Credits: 60

SEMESTER 2

Subject	Grade	Credits
Bible: Old Test. History	B	5
English: Comp & Grammer 9b	B	5
Geography 2	B	5
Animal Husbandry	B	5
Algebra 4	C	5
Latin 2	B	5
P.E.	A	5

Sem. 1 GPA: 2.83   Sem. 1 Credits: 35
Cum GPA: 3.29   Cum Credits: 95

Grade: 10   School Year: 2006/2007   Start Date: 08/12/2006   End Date: 05/23/2007

SEMESTER 1

Subject	Grade	Credits
Bible: The Poetry Books	A	5
English: American Literature 1	B	5
Modern U.S. History 1	C	5
Agricultural Studies	B	5
Trigonometry 1	C	5
Latin 3	B	5
P.E.	B	5

Sem. 1 GPA: 2.83   Sem. 1 Credits: 35
Cum GPA: 3.17   Cum Credits: 130

SEMESTER 2

Subject	Grade	Credits
Bible: The Prophets	A	5
English: American Literature 2	B	5
Modern U.S. History 2	B	5
Master Gardners	B	5
Trigonometry 2	C	5
Latin 4	B	5
P.E.	A	5

Sem. 1 GPA: 3.00   Sem. 1 Credits: 35
Cum GPA: 3.14   Cum Credits: 165

Grade: 11   School Year: 2007/2008   Start Date:09/02/2007   End Date: 08/25/2008

SEMESTER 1

Subject	Grade	Credits
Bible: The New Testament	A	5
English: English Literature 1	B	5
Modern World History 1	C	5
U.S. Government and Civics	C	5
Latin 5	B	5
Gourmet Cooking 1	A	5
P.E.	B	5

Sem. 1 GPA: 3.00   Sem. 1 Credits: 35
Cum GPA: 3.11   Cum Credits: 200

SEMESTER 2

Subject	Grade	Credits
Bible: Christan Discpleship	B	5
English: English Literature 2	A	5
Modern World History 2	B	5
Economics	B	5
Latin 6	A	5
Interior Design 1	B	5
P.E.	A	5

Sem. 1 GPA: 3.33   Sem. 1 Credits: 35
Cum GPA: 3.15   Cum Credits: 235

Graduation Requirements Complete: 08/25/2008   Passed CHSPE: May 2008
Enrolled in Anaheim Bible College   09/07/2008

An Introduction to Home Education, 12th Edition Revised, 2014

Glossary

Attendance Log or Attendance Record

Documentation of the days a student was present or absent from school. For homeschoolers, a " present" day would be any day for which you have documented education taking place.

Branches of Study

The required subjects which must be offered by private schools. For grades 1 - 6 they are: English, math, social sciences, science, fine arts, health, and physical education. For grades 7 - 12 they are English, math, social sciences, science, fine arts, health, parenting skills, physical education, foreign language, applied arts, and vocational education.

California High School Proficiency Exam (CHSPE)

An exam given to students who wish to graduate from high school early by showing they have already mastered the material expected of a 12 grade graduate. Students who pass the exam receive a "Certificate of Proficiency," which is equal to a California high school diploma.

Charter School

A public school which is organized by a group of teachers, community members, parents or others, and sponsored by an existing local public school board or county board of education. The specific goals and operating procedures are spelled out in the agreement between the board and the organizers. The school is freed from most of the requirements of the Education Code, but is subject to specific requirements for charter schools.

Christian Home Educators Association of California (CHEA)

The oldest and largest statewide home school organization in the United States, CHEA is a nonprofit ministry established to promote private Christian home education as an outstanding educational opportunity; to provide information, training, and support to the home education community; and to protect the God-given right of parents to direct the education and training of their children.

Correspondence School or Distance Learning

Historically, a correspondence school taught non-classroom students by mailing them lessons and exercises, which upon completion were returned to the school for grading. In the modern age, the Internet and e-mail have dramatically changed correspondence schools. The newer term "distance learning" encompasses both correspondence and online instruction.

Course of Study

As used in the Education Code, a list of subjects offered by a school. However, in practical usage, the term also means a list of subjects taken during a particular school year or taken by a particular student.

Cum or Cumulative File

Also called an Individual Pupil Record, this is a cumulative record of a student's school experience and follows him from school to school. The record contains such information as name, address, birth date, grades, etc.

Curriculum

Textbooks and other resources to aid the teacher in teaching.

Daily (or Dailies or Daily Log)

A record documenting what educational tasks were completed on a specific date. Usually included under each subject area are the textbooks used and the pages, concepts, or projects covered. This is not the same as a lesson plan, which is a proposed list of assignments; a daily is a record of what is actually completed.

Distance Education or Distance Learning

An educational program which teaches students from a distance, usually via internet, email, or correspondence.

Family Protection Ministries

The non-profit watchdog organization which monitors legislation, court cases, and government contacts to protect the legal status of private home education and parental rights issues.

General Education Development (GED)

A life-skills test to measure whether a student 18 years or older has learned enough to function in the adult world (e.g., get a job, pay bills, vote, etc.). Those who pass the exam receive a "Certificate of Equivalency" which is used in place of a high school diploma.

Home School Legal Defense Association (HSLDA)

Home School Legal Defense Association is a nonprofit advocacy organization established to defend and advance the constitutional right of parents to direct the education of their children and to protect family freedoms.

Independent Study Program (ISP)

A public school program which is similar to homeschooling in that the students do not attend a campus program. A public school employee supervises and has authority over the student and his schoolwork. This term used to be used within the private homeschool community to describe a school which enrolls homeschoolers. However, a recent court case implied that since the term is defined in the Education Code as a program supervised by public school officials, the term is not correctly used to describe similar programs in the private sector. Thus for private school programs the newer term is "private school satellite program" or PSP.

Individual Pupil Record

See Cum or Cumulative File

Lesson Plan

A lesson plan is a detailed strategy for pursuing your educational objectives. It generally lists assignments and projects to be completed by the student during the stated time period.

Private School Affidavit (PSA)

A document required to be filed annually with the state by private schools. It is sometimes called the "R-4" referring to the form number that used to appear on the form when it was distributed in paper format.

Private School Satellite Program (PSP)

A private school program which enrolls homeschool students. PSPs are commonly operated as either private businesses or as non-profit ministries. They may be associated with a private campus school or may be stand-alone programs with no campus. Formerly these programs were called "private ISPs."

R-4

See Private School Affidavit.

School Records

Records that are kept by and relate to a school, such as a course of study, faculty qualifications, etc. Contrast with cum files, which are records related to individual students.

Support Group

A group of home school families who meet together and typically participate in activities for mutual support. The individual families usually either establish their own private schools or join local PSPs — the support group does not operate as a school.

Teaching Records

Records kept by teachers documenting what was taught and how. These include daily lesson plans, unit study outlines, field trip journals, and teacher notes. Teaching records are the property of the teacher and are not included in a child's cumulative file.

Umbrella School or Umbrella Program

A generic term meaning any program or school that offers enrollment or instructional services to homeschool families. The term developed from the idea of providing a "covering" to allow the family to legally teach their children at home without establishing its own private school.

Index